THE PIRANDELLO COMMENTARIES

THE PIRANDELLO
COMMENTARIES
by
Eric Bentley

Northwestern University Press
Evanston, Illinois

Permission to print material from *The Playwright as Thinker* has been graciously provided by Harcourt Brace Jovanovich, Inc.
Permission to print material from *The Life of the Drama* has been graciously provided by Atheneum Publishers.
An earlier version of this collection appeared in *Pirandellian Studies* 1 (Winter 1985).

Northwestern University Press, Evanston, Illinois 60201

Library of Congress Catalog Card Number 86-61563

For Albert Bermel

"Suppose that, at the climax, when the marionette who is playing Orestes is about to avenge his father's death and kill his mother and Aegisthus, a little hole were torn in the paper sky above him? Orestes would still want his revenge, yet when he saw the hole, he would feel helpless. Orestes would become Hamlet! That's the difference between ancient tragedy and modern: a hole in a paper sky."

CONTENTS

Acknowledgments   ix

1986
Instead of a Preface   xi

1946
Pirandello and Modern Comedy   1

1952
Liolà and Other Plays   9

1954
Right You Are   25

1964
From *The Life of the Drama*   37

1966
Enrico IV   43

1968
Six Characters in Search of an Author   57

1971
The Life and Works of Luigi Pirandello   79

CONTENTS

1975
Gaspare Giudice's Biography   91

1986
"The Theatre against Itself"?   97

Appendix A: The Source of *Right You Are* (1954)   101

Appendix B: Bibliographical Notes (1986)   111

Index   115

ACKNOWLEDGMENTS

My attention was first called to Luigi Pirandello by student productions, at Oxford in or around 1936, of *Six Characters* and *To Clothe the Naked*. I knew at once that he would stay with me, though I did not learn what his theatrical presence really amounted to till I saw the Comédie-Française do *Right You Are* about a year later. It was this production that first emboldened me to write about the Maestro (1945–46), and when I came to direct a play of his, that play was *Right You Are* (Brattle Theatre, Cambridge, 1952).

Arguably there are only four masterpieces among Pirandello's many scintillating plays: *Liolà*, *Right You Are*, *Six Characters*, and *Enrico IV*, though I should be tempted to add *To Clothe the Naked* and several of the one acts. At that, the full force of even one of the masterpieces, *Enrico IV*, can be brought home only by a virtuoso actor. For me, this was Jean Vilar in the late forties.

What I'm saying is that my primary acknowledgment must be to those who showed me what Pirandello can be on stage, but I also learned a lot from Italian friends who not only improved my Italian but helped me understand Italy and its greatest modern playwright: especially the late Vito Pandolfi, Luciano Lucignani, Gerardo and Anne Guerrieri, Paolo Milano and Fabrizio Melano. Working with an Italian-American actor, Alfred Drake, on an important Pirandello role (Laudisi) was also a part of my education.

Friends in America who themselves write on theatre, and some of whom edit, or did edit, journals gave me encouragement—the most encouraging thing of all for a writer being publication, which those who could also gave: let me name Ed Doctorow, Robert W. Corrigan, Richard Schechner, Erika Munk, and Toby Cole.

ACKNOWLEDGMENTS

The essay in this book on *Six Characters* is the most detailed analysis I have ever written of a single play, but I, singly, did not write it. It grew out of a symposium organized by the late Dr. Philip Weissman; and an article (cited below) by Dr. Charles Kligerman had much to do with it; as had the comments of my constant friend and encourager, Albert Bermel.

My thanks to Walter Centuori, through whose initiative the present collection was put together, and to my colleagues of The Pirandello Society of America, whose president, Anne Paolucci, graciously dedicated her own book on Pirandello to me.

ERIC BENTLEY
NEW YORK CITY, JANUARY, 1986

INSTEAD OF A PREFACE

Why has Pirandello been so important to you? I am asked. The book itself—this book—must be the answer. Instead of adding a lengthy introduction, I'd just like to quote part of a discussion I had with a Voice of America interviewer on the subject of *The Life of the Drama*, my principal book on drama as a whole:

VOICE OF AMERICA: Is it possible to encapsulate such a large book for us here?

EB: I should hope not. What I can do is cite what surprised me most about it when it was done. My friends had said it would be an elaboration of Brecht's ideas. I myself thought it might be Aristotle's *Poetics* as rephrased by a Freudian—I was being "analyzed" at the time. What surprised me was that the philosophy of theatre in my book wasn't either Brecht (my father) or Freud (my guru in those years) but Pirandello, one of a number of Europeans I had translated. He saw life as role playing.

VOICE OF AMERICA: But by now isn't that idea a commonplace of psychiatry?

EB: Except that the psychiatrists earn their money by promising *a release* from role playing. You discover the real you, remember? Nothing different there from what you learned at mother's knee! The different thing in Pirandello was: *all* life is role playing. No way out. All the men and women *merely* players. . . .

VOICE OF AMERICA: But is that true? Or perhaps we should only ask: did you *take* it to be true?

EB: I took it to be an explanation of theatre, or as near to such an explanation as we shall ever get. Theatre provides an image of life, *the* image of life, because *life is a theatre.*

INSTEAD OF A PREFACE

VOICE OF AMERICA: "All the world's a stage." That's not Pirandello, that's Shakespeare.

EB: Shakespeare didn't mean it. Pirandello did. For Shakespeare, or maybe just for his Jaques who says the line, the notion is merely illustrative. At best a comparison: life reminds one of drama in one or two vivid ways. No problem is seen therein. In Pirandello, it is all problem, even agony—that one cannot escape from play-acting. If there is any truth in that, then theatre embodies the profoundest pain and conflict—a whole destiny.

VOICE OF AMERICA: Then you do believe Pirandellianism is true?

EB: Obviously I'm convinced there's something to it. Much. But what I was most convinced of was that it brought me to the center of my particular subject, the subject of my life's intellectual-spiritual effort . . . Life is dramatic: that is a very general notion but there are many fascinating specifics to it—in the details of role playing, of drama building. Drama is important because all human beings dramatize all the time. It seems to be the only way to reach out, to try to grasp, to visualize oneself and others, to recapitulate the past, to plan the future. Scenarios. Enactments. A dramatist is just a man who makes a *work of art* out of constructs which all of us put together inartistically.

VOICE OF AMERICA. Very conclusive.

EB. Oh dear, conclusiveness is something Pirandello didn't approve of—except maybe in politics. In his art he embraced the inconclusive, the tremendous inconclusiveness of things, *la tremenda sconclusione*. So let me quote him on this topic. I can't find the quote in his collected works: I found it in a periodical called *La preparazione*, dated 1909. And in this passage it seems better to translate *sconclusione* as *discontinuity*:

> I love and admire souls that are discontinuous, unquiet, in a state of almost continuous flow, souls that scorn to coagulate or rigidify in this or that predetermined shape. And among the books I most frequently return to, I love two above the rest: *The Life and Opinions of Tristram Shandy*, the most discontinuous of all novels ever written, and the *Hamlet* of Shakespeare, which Goethe called an insoluble problem precisely because of its tremendous discontinuity. The just and the unjust, the ingenuous and the deceitful, the prudent and the rash, all meet with the same end, and no one triumphs except accident.

For someone of English background like myself, this passage makes contact with the Italian Maestro easy and congenial. And everything does flow from those two works: *Enrico IV* from *Hamlet*, *Six Characters* from *Tristram Shandy* . . . .

PIRANDELLO AND MODERN COMEDY

Since Shaw and Wilde no dramatist has written first-rate drawing-room comedies. The best have been by our Maughams and Behrmans and Bernsteins. Writers have been turning from the formality of the drawing room toward a grotesqueness which, in its nearness to *commedia dell'arte* or to Aristophanes, may seem more primitive, yet which, in its psychological depth and intricacy, may well be more sophisticated. Strindberg himself sometimes achieved comedy by giving a quick twist to one of his own tragic themes. Wedekind aimed at tragedy, but by the novel method of using almost exclusively comic materials, thus reversing the technique of Strindberg's comedies. In Italy *il teatro del grottesco* arose. Its spokesman Luigi Chiarelli said: "It was impossible [in the years immediately preceding 1914] to go to the theater without meeting languid, loquacious granddaughters of Marguerite Gautier or Rosa Bernd, or some tardy follower of Oswald or Cyrano. The public dropped sentimental tears and left the playhouse weighed down in spirit. The next evening, however, it rushed in numbers to acclaim a naughty skit like *The Pills of Hercules*, in order to reestablish its moral and social equilibrium." From Chiarelli's scorn for the New Drama, already old, of Dumas and Hauptmann, Ibsen and Rostand, came his own play, *The Mask and the Face*. The year of its premiere—1916—was the year Luigi Pirandello embarked on his second career: that of playwriting.

Right You Are (1917) has often been regarded as the quintessential Pirandello. The basis of the play is some sort of "bourgeois tragedy," something that would have stirred the audiences of the old-new drama which Chiarelli had laughed at. The domestic unhappiness of a husband, a wife, and a mother makes up the tragic triangle. A commentator named Laudisi is the *raisonneur* à la Dumas.

1

The peculiar thing about the situation in this domestic tragedy is that we do not know what it is: a fact that is as much second nature to Pirandellians as it is disconcerting to others. The peculiar thing about the *raisonneur* is that instead of giving us the correct view of the tragedy he tells us that all views are equally correct. But then, according to Pirandello, *this* is the correct view.

The man lives with his wife on the top floor of a tenement while the mother lives at his expense in a lavish apartment. The wife never leaves the tenement, and the mother never goes nearer the daughter than the yard below from which she shouts up to her. This state of affairs not unnaturally sets tongues wagging. Asked for an explanation, the husband says the mother is deluded. She thinks the wife is her daughter, though actually she is the husband's second wife. Her daughter, his first wife, died, though the mother dare not believe it. . . . We are settling down to believe this version of the story when we hear from the mother an equally convincing version. The son is deluded. He has never recovered from the delusion that his wife died, and they have had to let him marry her again under the impression that she was another person.

Neither mother nor husband seems to have an axe to grind. Each is solicitous for the other's good. Each has a good reason for strange conduct. The mother needs to see her daughter often and must pay her visits. The husband must keep the mother in the street so that she shall not discover her error. Pirandello is at great pains to balance the two interpretations exactly, to tug our feelings now this way, now that, now up, now down, on the alarming switchback of his thinking. We may think ourselves on the right track, for example, when the husband, untrue to his story, is furiously angry with the old lady and tries to convince her that his wife is not her daughter. But, as soon as she leaves, his rage subsides. He was just play-acting, he tells us, to confirm her impression—so necessary to her peace of mind—that he is mad.

In the end the wife herself is summoned to unravel the mystery. She says: "I am the daughter of Signora Frola [the mother], and I am the second wife of Signor Ponza [the husband]." The *raisonneur* of the play, who already has told us that there is no one true version of the story but that all versions are equally true, steps forward, and his peals of laughter end the play. Whereupon one school of critics praises Pirandello for his profound "philosophy of relativity," and another condemns him as "too cerebral"—only "mentally dramatic," as George Jean Nathan has it, *Right You Are* being "written for intelligent blind men." The critical boxing ring would seem to be set for a bout concerning the drama of ideas.

2

Like Shaw, Pirandello has not been averse to the report that his drama is all intellect—no man minds being thought a mighty brain—and here are some of his words: "People say that my drama is obscure and they call it cerebral drama. The new drama possesses a distinct character from the old: whereas the latter had as its basis passion, the former is the expression of the intellect. . . . The public formerly were carried away only by plays of passion, whereas now they rush to see intellectual works."

Such is the Pirandello legend. Around every great man there grows a legend which, whether fostered by himself or not, is always a distortion, sometimes a gross distortion of his real nature—if we may assume the existence of so un-Pirandellian an entity. The omission which I disingenuously made in the above quotation from Pirandello is a casual remark that happens to be more revealing than the pontificality of the rest. It is this sentence: "One of the novelties that I have given to the modern drama consists in converting the intellect into passion." Let us discount here the claim to originality. Strindberg had already perfected the art referred to. A succession of dramatists from Vigny on had announced a new drama of thought and intellect. The essence of Pirandello is not his intellectuality. It is his conversion of the intellect into passion. Perhaps Strindberg had done that too; it is the theory behind his naturalistic tragedies; yet in Strindberg passion summons intellect to work its will, while in Pirandello passion and intellect torture each other and join in a mutual failure. The quintessence of Pirandellianism is this peculiar relation of intellect to feeling.

Ostensibly Pirandello's plays and novels are about the relativity of truth, multiple personality, and the different levels of reality. But it is neither these subjects nor—precisely—his treatment of them that constitutes Pirandello's individuality. The themes grow tiresome after a time, and those who find nothing else in Pirandello give him up as a bad job. The novelist Franz Kafka was long neglected because his work also gave the impression of philosophic obsession and willful eccentricity. Then another and deeper Kafka was discovered. Another and deeper Pirandello awaits discovery.

Before he can be discovered the perpetual "cerebration" concerning truth, reality, and relativity will have to be set on one side. At face value the argument of *Right You Are* is that, since both mother and husband give a contradictory but equally plausible account of the same events, and since the daughter jumbles the two incomprehensibly, there is no objectively true version of the story. This is a *non sequitur*. All events can be reported in different ways. This might only mean that some reports must be wrong, not that there is no right view.

3

There is nothing in the plot of *Right You Are* to indicate that there can be no correct version of the story. The unusual thing is that we do not know what it is. This is very Pirandellian—not only, however, in that it is used to bolster a rather confusing, if not confused, discussion of truth, but also because it leads us to what we might venture to think is the real Pirandello.

The wife's longest speech—of three sentences—is as follows: "And what can you want of me now, after all this, ladies and gentlemen? In our lives as you see there is something which must be concealed. Otherwise the remedy which our love for each other has found cannot avail." The concealment which leads on the superficial, pseudo-metaphysical level to a discussion of truth is here very differently associated. There *is* a true version of the story but it must not be known lest the lives of three people concerned be shattered. But, someone will protest, could not Pirandello use the prerogative of the omniscient author and tell *us* without telling the characters what the remedy is which their love has found? He could. But his refusal to do so is more to his purpose. The truth, Pirandello wants to tell us again and again, is concealed, *concealed*, CONCEALED! It is not his business to uncover the problem and solve it for us as in a French *pièce à thèse*. The solution of the problem, the cure for these sick human beings, is to leave their problem unsolved and unrevealed. The unmasker of illusions is at best a Gregers Werle, at worst one of the gossips of *Right You Are*. On the superficial level Pirandello is protesting against the spurious helpfulness of the scandalmonger, the prying reporter, and the amateur psychoanalyst; at a deeper level he is asking that the human soul be left a little territory of its own—which was also one of the themes of Kafka.

As for dramaturgy, if the "remedy" were explained, the play would inevitably be built around this keystone of the whole problem. Pirandello could not afford—whatever the inducements—to have the emphasis so disturbed. He wants to accent the refusal to search for a keystone. So he has his *raisonneur* argue that there is no keystone—an argument which sticks in people's minds as if it were the substance of the play. Actually the play is not about thinking but about suffering, a suffering that is only increased by those who give understanding and enquiry precedence over sympathy and help. Pirandello took from the *teatro del grottesco* or from his own fiction the antithesis of mask and face, the mask being the outward form, the face being the suffering creature. At its crudest this is the theme of the clown with a tender heart. Already in Chiarelli the mask and the face had, however, the broader meaning of the social form, identified with tyranny, and the individual soul which it sought to crush. In his best-known plays Pi-

4

randello elaborates on this antithesis. We see a central group of people who are "real." They suffer, and need help, not analysis. Around these are grouped unreal busybodies who can only look on, criticize, and hinder. In *To Clothe the Naked*, which is the first Pirandello play to read since it does not lead one off on the false trail of relativity and truth, the mystery *is* dissolved, as in *Right You Are* it is not, and the result is the destruction of the protagonist. Note that this mystery, constituted by the illusions without which the heroine could not live, is not the Mask. The Mask is the social and anti-human tyranny of, for example, a novelist for whom the heroine's unhappy lot is grist to the mill. The Mask is the interference of the mechanical, the external, the static, the philosophical, with our lives. Thus not only the smug novelist of *To Clothe the Naked* and not only the disingenuous truth seekers of *Right You Are* are the Mask. Pirandello himself—and every novelist and playwright—is the Mask. His material is the flux of suffering; his art stops the flow; its stasis is at once its glory—in immortalizing the moment—and its limitation, since life, being essentially fluid, is inevitably misrepresented by art. In drama, life wears a double mask: the mask imposed by the dramatist and that imposed by stage production. Three plays are devoted to this fact. In the best of them—*Six Characters in Search of an Author*—the three levels of reality are played off against one another throughout, and a fourth level is implied when we find one character judging another by what he happened to be doing on one shameful occasion, in other words by one isolated fact, which, wrongly taken as typical, becomes a Mask on the face of the real man. What if all our characterizations are like this? Just as we found, Pirandello argues, that there is no objective truth, so we find also that there are no individuals. In the one case we have only a number of versions or opinions. In the other we have only a succession of states of mind and being.

Exactly as in the matter of truth, so in the analysis of character the extreme conclusion is a *reductio ad absurdum* too barren to be the real motive force of such powerful works as Pirandello's. His characters are effective not in direct relation to these conceptions, but because these conceptions enable him to suggest beneath the Mask of the physical presence the steady ache of suffering humanity. What a pessimist Pirandello is! says someone. Certainly. But again the point is not his philosophy—of relativity, personality, or pessimism—it is his power to conceal behind the intellectual artillery barrage the great armies of fighters and the yet greater hordes of noncombatants and refugees. Pirandello is a pessimist. So also must many of the people of Europe be, people who have lived through the extraordinary vicissitudes of the twentieth century, uncomprehending, passively suffering. Modern people may be no more passive and uncomprehending than their ancestors; but surely they are more aware of their helplessness. Even as Proust speaks for the passive semi-aristocrats whom our new order has swept out of existence, so Pirandello, like Kafka, like Chaplin, speaks not for the aware and class-conscious proletarian but for the unaware, in-between, black-coated scapegoat.

All this is in *Right You Are*. In a note to the director of the play one might write as follows:

"Make a marked distinction between the enquirers into the story, who are a sort of chorus representing what Pirandello regards as the Mask, and the three 'real people' involved in the domestic tragedy. The Three are typical people of a middle-class tragedy in that they express grief and arouse pity without terror. Note how Pirandello's initial descriptions of the characters and his subsequent stage directions stress alike the genuineness and acuteness of their sufferings.

"Now the odd thing is that the wholly sad theme is placed in a satiric frame. Since this contrast, already familiar to you in the *teatro del grottesco*, *is* the play, you had best be careful to secure the exact balance that is needed. The Three must act with unmitigated and uninterrupted pathetic force. But the Chorus—as we may call the other characters—must never enter into their sufferings. They must be as detached as a callous doctor at a deathbed. They must not, out of consideration of their Three colleagues, play down their own frivolity any more than the Three must soften their agony in order to come closer—as there is a natural tendency to do—to the mood of the Chorus. Only if the contrast between the two groups is kept sharp will the effect of the grotesque be attained. Otherwise the effect will be of blurred incongruity.

"You already understand how and why this bourgeois tragedy differs from tradition in not revealing its true nature. That is a primary irony which your production can point up by making the alternation of explanations go snipsnap so that the brilliance is its own justification. Otherwise your audience will regard all this as the lumbering preparation for a denouement which, after all, never takes place. An almost equally important irony is that between the celebrated 'cerebral' dialogue of Pirandello and the deep agony which—as your Three must make clear—is the core of the action. The irony is more than the contrast between the Three and the others. The Three actually join in the intricate analysis of cause and effect, motive and act, which is the constant subject of discussion. The point is that these analyses are not 'coldly intellectual.' They are positively maniacal. (You might look up Pirandello's essay on humor where he maintains that the humorist

6

takes a wild pleasure in tearing things to pieces by analysis.) By its maniacal quality the 'cerebration' enters into relationship with the agony, a relationship at once logical and psychological.

"You recall how in *Cyrano de Bergerac* Rostand rendered Hugoesque tragedy palatable by making it over into a tough-jointed tragi-comedy. The grotesque contrasts of *Right You Are* might be regarded as Pirandello's way of making 'bourgeois tragedy' work—by making it over into a tough-textured comedy. Perhaps comedy is not the best word for such a play, but then you as a practical man are less interested in that question than in the correct interpretation of the play whatever its generic name. For you the significance of Pirandello's version of bourgeois tragedy is that it sets the audience at a distance, preserving them both from tears and from boredom. Do not be shocked when they laugh *with* your Chorus *against* the Three or when they are amused with Laudisi the *raisonneur* when perhaps weeping would seem more in order. Their laughter is significant. For one thing it is what enables them to stomach the unmixed horror of Pirandellian diet. It is not stupid laughter. Pirandello has 'comedified' his tale. If the laughter he arouses prompts an unflattering interpretation of human nature, that is intended. The old theatrical business, at which you are adept, of mingling laughter and tears was never more calculated, more intricate, more meaningful, or more depressing than here.

"Accentuate then—do not soften—the clashes of sound and color of which the play is composed. If you let it work, you will find the whole thing ultra-theatrical. I should say: if you let *them* work, for a Pirandello play is made up of actors, not of props and scenery. That must be why our friend Mr. Nathan thought it was written for blind men. But remember that actors—especially the actors of the *commedia dell'arte* whose skill Pirandello wished to revive—once were, and can be again, the main part of the show. Tell your actors to let go. Have them shout, swagger, gesticulate—at least in the earlier rehearsals. For you have to get them to act and talk instead of strolling and muttering like mannequins with a pin loose. And if they perform their roles from outside instead of pretending to *be* the people who are not people, Pirandello would be better served. As you know, he called all his plays Naked Masks—not naked faces. Let your actors remember that. Naked Masks—a violent oxymoron indeed! Is not such a figure of speech a pointer, for you and the rest of us, to the strange genius of its author?"

LIOLÀ *AND OTHER PLAYS*

1

A generation ago there was, notoriously, a literature of ideas. Most of it, like most literature of all movements, was bad; and fashion, which elevates the bad to the level of the good, subsequently turns its back on bad and good alike. Only if there is a body of readers interested in merit as such can anything like justice be done.

Such readers will rescue the better literature of ideas from beneath the fashionable ideas about it. Even authors like Ibsen and Shaw, who are by no means unread, need rescuing from ideas about their ideas. How much the more so Pirandello, who is suffering fashionable rejection without ever having had—outside Italy—widespread fashionable acceptance! I have met persons who rejected him because of his "tiresome ideas" without being able to give me even their own version of what these ideas are. Pirandello needs rescuing from the very lack of ideas about his ideas.

It is true that too much of Pirandello, and Pirandello criticism, remains untranslated. The untranslated essay *"L'umorismo"* ("Humor") contains all his principal ideas (especially its Second Part). The untranslated later plays are especially full of theory. The untranslated essays of Adriano Tilgher (especially "Il Teatro di Luigi Pirandello" in *Studi sul teatro contemporaneo*) are the standard exposition from the point of view of the famous ideas. However, I submit that the ideas offer no real difficulty. They are old ideas, good old ideas,* some of

---

*The background of Pirandello's ideas can be looked at in several ways, e.g., (1) as belonging to age-old traditions that lead us back through, say, Pascal to Empedocles and

which would take us back to Pirandello's fellow-countrymen Empedo-cles and Gorgias. It was Pascal, not Pirandello, who first said: "There is no man who differs more from another than he does from himself at another time." Illusion and reality—the "mix up" of illusion and reali-ty—is so far from being a peculiarly Pirandellian theme as to be per-haps the main theme of literature in general.

"No," says the more knowledgeable reader, "it is not the ideas that give trouble. It's that we can't see why certain of them mattered so much to Pirandello. Always the *same* ideas! *'Oh, Dio mio, ma questo girar sempre sullo stesso pernio!'*—as he himself has his critics say. 'Oh, good heavens, this harping always on the same string!' More impor-tant: we can't see why these ideas should matter much to *us*."

Obviously this reader can't mean that Pirandello—in his essay on humor, say—does not make a strong enough case for his ideas, in the sense that a lawyer or a logician makes a case. An artist, and no one was more aware of it than Pirandello, makes his ideas matter by ren-dering them artistically active: that is, by giving them the life of his chosen form in his chosen medium. The question for us here, then, is whether Pirandello's ideas become active in the dramatic form.

In reconsidering Pirandello today, fifteen years after his death, the first play to read is *Liolà*. It loses more than other plays in translation, but perhaps enough of the original comes through to remove the anti-Pirandello prejudice. It is a play that lives by an evident loveliness. Sic-ily is a land of golden light, scarcely of this world, and Agrigento, with its Greek temples, its proud position above Porto Empedocle and the Mediterranean, and its isolation from both the merchants of Palermo and the tourists of Taormina, is perhaps the most charming spot on the island. Without any scene-painting whatsoever, and without (even in the Sicilian text) any attempt to create "poetic" peasant dialogue, Pi-randello has contrived to let in the light and distill the essence of the charm.

If it especially commends itself to those who love Sicily, the play has a quality all can appreciate, the more so for its rarity both in life and

---

Gorgias; (2) as deriving from whatever Pirandello had absorbed from German idealis-tic philosophy when he was a student in Bonn; (3) as deriving from German literature, especially from the drama of the Romantic school (a possible model for *Six Characters* would be Tieck's *Puss in Boots*); (4) as belonging to topics much discussed in turn-of-the-century Italy (as for example in books cited by Pirandello himself such as *Le fin-zioni dell'anima* by Giovanni Marchesini and *Segni dei tempi* by Gaetano Negri); (5) as paralleling contemporary Austrian literature, and specifically certain works by Ar-thur Schnitzler, such as *The Green Cockatoo*, and by Hugo von Hofmannsthal, such as his articles on Pirandello's favorite actress, Eleanora Duse. (Franz Rauhut has shown how Pirandello lifted passages from Marchesini.)

art today, and that is joy. High spirits and hilarity we can on occasion manage; in the theatre they are *de rigueur*; in real life they have their allotted place. But joy—as an actor would say—"there is nothing harder to do." Not even ecstasy. For ecstasy is extreme and preternatural, and that is in our line. Joy is "hard" for being pure and delicate, but no less "hard" for having its feet on the ground. It is bliss without otherworldliness. It lies tantalizingly in between the extremes of beatitude and bestiality, which are increasingly the postulates of our world. *Liolà* is a play for the 1950s. Amid the spurious apocalyptics of the few and the genuine hysteria of the many—so far the only spiritual manifestations of the atomic age—anything that recalls us to sanity is welcome. Pirandello's tidings of great joy are the best "message" any theatrical manager of today could find.

Liolà, to be sure, is Pirandello on holiday: he made one of his short trips back home to the island and dashed off the play in about one week. It is a dream, if you wish, but in no Celtic twilight or Maeterlinckian mist: it is all actual; it is all concrete. Sicily is like that: the African sun shines, the hard rock takes on the soft color of honey, the trees are laden with almonds and oranges, and vagabonds sing. Granted, Pirandello picked from this reality just those particulars that suited his mood and intention. The village could be the same village as in *Cavalleria rusticana*. Although Pirandello's mood and intention are different from Verga's, he has not overlooked reality. If he has dreamed himself away from the problems of Agrigento in 1916, it is back into the Agrigento of an earlier day. The breath of a happy paganism is felt in his comedy, which is the last Sicilian pastoral.

The greatest single creation of the piece is Liolà himself, from whom joy flows as from a fountain:

> Last night I slept the sleep I love,
> My cabin roof the stars above,
> A bit of earth, it was my bed,
> And there were thistles 'neath my head.
> Hunger and thirst and sorrow's sting,
> They touch me not: for I can sing!
> My heart, it jumps for joy: I sing!
> Of all the earth and sea I'm king.
> I wish to all men health and sun,
> To me may lovely lasses run!
> May curly children round me gather
> With an old lady like my mother!

And Liolà is a holiday creation, a truancy on Pirandello's part, an exception to the rules of the Maestro's craft. He is one of the few gay characters in Pirandello, and perhaps the only positive one. By positive I mean morally positive, being an agent, not merely a victim; hammer, not merely anvil. There is positive will in Henry IV and in Baldovino (of *The Pleasure of Honesty*), but Life sweeps in like a flood and decides the issue. Neither of these protagonists is, like Liolà, master of his fate. He is master of his fate without being a hero, and that by steadfastly refusing to do what other Pirandello characters do: let himself be exploited. This fact is firmly fixed in Pirandello's plot.

The story is essentially that of Tuzza's attempted revenge on Mita, who has both the rich husband (Simone) and the gallant lover (Liolà) whom Tuzza would like to have. Tuzza gets herself pregnant by Liolà and then arranges for Simone to pretend that the child is his. This he is eager to do because he has never been able to beget an heir. Mita will therefore fall from grace, and Tuzza become the mistress of Simone's household.

The snag is that Liolà will not stand for it. He warns Tuzza and her aunt: "Look, I wouldn't like to commit an outrage. But I also wouldn't like others to commit an outrage and make use of me." When the plotters ignore the warning, he decides to make Mita pregnant too, so that she can reassume her wifely dignity. (For Simone will now disown Tuzza's child and claim Mita's.) The turning-point of the action is therefore Liolà's seduction of Mita. Urging her to cuckold Simone, he uses the same language he had used before: "No, no, this outrage must not stand, Mita! . . . The wretch mustn't make use of me to bring about your ruin!" He will not be made use of.

Were the opposite the case, as it is with all Pirandello's other characters, the story would not have a happy ending; it would be a normal, unhappy Pirandello play. And indeed, having granted that the character of Liolà, as it works out both in the action and in the tone of the dialogue, turns everything around, one must insist a little on the converse of the proposition: save for a single, central reversal of values, *Liolà* is characteristically Pirandellian. It would be hasty, for example, to congratulate the author on having forgotten for once the famous ideas. On the contrary: we can learn from this play what his ideas are.

The play is about appearance and reality, and shows, in what readers have always regarded as Pirandello's characteristically tricky fashion, that reality is not more real than appearance. Further, there are real appearances and—merely apparent appearances. And just as appearance may be more real than reality, so merely apparent appearance may be more real than real appearance.

Now, the point is that though this sounds like an undergraduate discussion of Bishop Berkeley, in Pirandello's context it is concrete and clear. To appear to be a father is enough for Uncle Simone: appearance will establish his paternity more surely than actually having done the deed. Strictly speaking, however, he does *not* appear to be a father; for the whole town knows the truth. He only appears to appear to be the father. That he appears to be the father is a kind of social pact or legal fiction.

And here a distinction is made. Tuzza excludes Uncle Simone from the pact by actually telling him what has happened and thus preventing him from pretending to himself that the child is his. Mita doesn't make this mistake. It matters nothing that others shout the news in his face. That is unofficial gossip. The understanding, the apparent appearance, is that he is the father of Mita's child. And it is this appearance of an appearance, this shadow of a shadow, that brings back into Mita's grasp the solid realities of Simone's wealth and power.

> TUZZA: You managed it better than I did. You have facts on your side. I
> have—words.
> MITA: Only words? I don't see it.
> AUNT CROCE: Words, *words*, WORDS! The deceit people see in *us* is no
> deceit at all. The real deceit is in you—but no one sees it. . . . You
> have your husband again. You deceived him, but he gives you shel-
> ter. Whereas my daughter wouldn't deceive her uncle, oh no: she
> threw herself at his feet and wept like Mary Magdalene!
> UNCLE SIMONE: That's true, that's true!
> AUNT CROCE: You see! He says so himself—he who was the cause of all
> the trouble—just so he could boast before the whole village . . . .
> MITA: And you let him do that, Aunt Croce? Come now, at the cost of
> your daughter's honor? But I agree with you: the deceit is where no
> one sees it—in my husband's riches—which you wished to take over
> at the cost of your own shame!

Considering how the theme of reality and illusion is embedded in the action, particularly in such a passage as the one just quoted, we see that it is not important for itself only, but also as referring to the concrete and indeed humble circumstances of human society. Brought up in the liberal tradition, we expect an author who, like Pirandello, "exposes illusions" to "champion reality," whereas he is content to leave the deceit "in Mita," to accept the veil of illusion. In "Humor," published eight years before *Liolà* was conceived, he had written:

> The harder the struggle for life and the more one's weakness is felt, the greater becomes the need for mutual deception. [The word is *inganno*, as in *Liolà*.] The simulation of force, honesty, sympathy, prudence—in short, of every virtue, and of that greatest virtue, veracity—is

a form of adjustment, an effective instrument of struggle. The "humorist" at once picks out such various simulations; amuses himself by unmasking them; is not indignant about them: he simply is that way!

And while the sociologist describes social life as it presents itself to external observation, the humorist, being a man of exceptional intuition, shows—nay, reveals—that appearances are one thing and the consciousness of the people concerned, in its inner essence, another. And yet people "lie psychologically" even as they "lie socially." And this lying to ourselves—living, as we do, on the surface and not in the depths of our being—is a result of the social lying. The mind that gives back its own reflection is a solitary mind, but our internal solitude is never so great that suggestions from the communal life do not break in upon it with all the fictions and transferences that characterize them.*

Mita is not mocked. She needs her "simulations" in her "struggle for life," in her struggle against society; and Pirandello is "not indignant about them." If he is conservative and "Latin" in defending established conventions against the skeptic, he is liberal and "Protestant" in his feeling that society is an enemy against which the individual, in his "inner essence," needs protection. As much as in any of the libertarian literature of the nineteenth century, public opinion in Pirandello is uniformly the opinion of a stupid, heartless, inquisitive outer world. One need not refer back to Stendhal or to the English legend of Mrs. Grundy. Pirandello had met Mrs. Grundy at home and in real life long before he could have met her abroad or in literature.

Pirandello's "liberalism" is protected by his "conservatism": his individuals are protected in their struggle against society by illusion, convention, mendacity, pretense. Liolà knows this, even if the proverbial, gnomic language he finds to express it shows that such wisdom is for him intuitive and traditional, not arrived at by study, discussion, or even observation. He knows it without fully knowing that he knows it, for he is civilized without being educated, a thing that people who are educated without being civilized find hard to grasp. He has the smiling wisdom of an old culture. With his bones if not with his head he knows that life is ironical. The whole play is in one of his first and most casual remarks: "Pretending is virtue, and if you can't pretend, you can't be king." I have spoken already of his seduction of Mita as the turning-point of the plot. His chief argument is the very fulcrum of the theme. It is that to bring everything out in the open is foolish. "Beatings and screechings, the lawyer, the Deputy, a separation? . . . Who will believe it? Well, possibly they all will. Except him. He'll never believe it—for the good reason that he doesn't wish to." If we need a

*Luigi Pirandello, *Saggi* (Milan: Mondadori, 1939), p. 163.

dignified antecedent for this, it will not be *An Enemy of the People* but *The Wild Duck*.

2

I have asserted that Liolà himself is the exceptional feature of the play that bears his name, and that otherwise it is characteristically Pirandellian. Pirandello, indeed, makes of him an exception not only in the canon of his own work, but also in life; Liolà does not belong to modern society, to the bourgeois world. Interesting as his antagonism to private property may be, he stands outside the class system, and breathes the spirit of an earlier day. He can be independent only at the cost of being a vagabond with few demands to make on life. Otherwise what would his wisdom avail him?

Even before he left Sicily, Pirandello must have known there was no future in such an ideal, and when he got to Rome he must have found there was not even a present. The great bulk of Pirandello's work bears witness to the sadness of a spirit that reaches back to pagan joy and Garibaldian heroism, but is confronted with the unheroic joylessness of the urban middle class. It is easy to understand why there is only one Liolà, still easier to overlook the typicality of his play and the correlative fact that the other plays draw their energy from the same sources, and not from books of philosophy and psychology.

Not least the play that is the most famous statement of Pirandello's "relativism"—*Right You Are*. In this play, preeminently, we see the struggle for life in its inner essence, life in the private depths. The struggle is caused, or exacerbated, by the desire of other people to know the truth about a certain family. Pirandello maintains the view, we are told, that truth is relative and subjective, the joke being that they know the truth already because whatever seems so to each of them is so. One would think the play philosophical and the philosophy cynical, but what is this love of truth that Pirandello condemns? It is no Socratic dedication, it is Mrs. Grundy's nosiness, it is the idle curiosity of Ciuzza, Luzza, and Nela, which has gained in malignancy as it has risen in social station. This love of truth is the pseudo-religion of the bureaucratic fact, on the altars of which men are sacrificed to paper and typewriters: the recourse to documents in Acts Two and Three parallels Aunt Gesa's rushing to the lawyer in *Liolà*.

In *Liolà*, to stick to the terms of the play itself, deception (*inganno*) leads to outrage (*infamia*), whereupon a remedy (*rimedio*) is found, not by exposure of the deception, but by another and larger deception. The human content of the larger deception is not, however, deception itself, or evil, but humanity, the wisdom of Liolà. This *gaia scienza*, I have said, would have no place in the bourgeois plays, of which *Right You Are* is one of the first. Here there is no active mastery of the situation. There is passive suffering, and an effort to compose matters through affection. When all else has been blasted away, kindness, like joy, is the pearl of great price. For Liolà's serene mastery, it is at any rate a handy substitute. Mother-in-law, son-in-law, and wife know it is their most precious possession, their one sure, real possession.

The old lady warns the truth-lovers early on: "And why is it necessary then to torment him with this investigation of his family life?" Ponza explains to the well-wishers how much ill they do: "I beg your pardon for this sad spectacle I've had to present before all you ladies and gentlemen to remedy the evil that, without wanting, without knowing, you are doing to this unhappy woman with your compassion." He cries out to them in pain: ". . . I cannot tolerate this fierce, relentless investigation of my private life. In the end it will compromise—irreparably destroy—a labor of love which is costing me much pain, much sacrifice." The old lady cries out too: "You think to help me and you do me so much harm!" The veiled wife is even more explicit: "There is a misfortune here, as you see, which must remain hidden because only in this way can the remedy that compassion has found avail."

The *rimedio* comes to us, as in *Liolà*, as the largest deception of all; *we* feel as much deceived as the people on stage. Yet again its content is humanity, this time in the shape of *carità, pietà*. While, certainly, the entrance of the veiled wife carries this "parable" beyond the bounds of realism, we are under no obligation to believe, as many have, that she is Truth itself. If she must have a capital letter, she is Love. Just how her birth certificate reads does not matter; she has lost her separate interests, her separate existence, in devotion to the others; she exists only in the mother and the husband. This alone, this love and theirs, is true: the rest?—you can have it your own way.

Enrico IV and the "trilogy of the theatre in the theatre" (*Six Characters, Each in His Own Way*, and *Tonight We Improvise*) represent a development of this "system" rather than a break with it. In *Enrico IV* the Pirandellian version of illusion and reality has crystallized in his celebrated confrontation of form and life. The kinetic pattern is still deception, outrage, and remedy by larger deceit. The spatial pattern is still a center of suffering and a periphery of busybodies.

To Pirandello, form increasingly meant artistic form, and artistic form increasingly meant dramatic form. Theatre and life are the theme. His standard version of it is the spatial pattern of the Sicilian village, a drama of suffering and a crowd of onlookers: Tuzza and all Agrigento looking on; the Ponza-Frola trio and the whole provincial capital looking on; Henry IV, a spectacle for his friends and his servants; the six characters, a drama to amaze actors and stage manager; Delia Morello, with her double out front and actors on stage discussing the author; Mommina, dying in a play within a play while singing in a play within a play within a play.

The heterodox form of *Six Characters* is thus no freak, and has nothing to do with the bohemian experimentalism of the twenties with which people still associate it. It closely corresponds to Pirandello's sense of life, and is but an extension of a pattern he had, as we have seen, used before. In *Liolà* and *Right You Are*, he juggles with reality and appearance, interchanging them, subdividing them, mixing them, always urgently aware of different degrees or levels of illusion. Having established a level midway between the audience and the essential drama—that of the spectator characters—he could go a step farther and use the device of the play within a play, which is all that we mean when we talk of the play's formal heterodoxy.

Some think that Pirandello's turning from *Liolà* (and the short story) to more ambitious forms of drama was all to the bad: the more he tried to be a thinker, the less he succeeded in being an artist. Finding a Liolà giving place to a Laudisi, one certainly fears the worst. To give one's wisdom to a spectator character, a *raisonneur*, might well mean the weakening of plot and the dilution of dialogue.

Yet *Right You Are* has a strong plot and (in the original) a concise dialogue. Laudisi does not stand at the center of the action because Pirandello has reserved that place for his three sufferers. Laudisi's talk is a commentary; its force is not direct—cannot therefore be judged in quotation—but derives from ironic interaction with the main business. He is a spectator character. Pirandello is painting the portrait of a spectator at the drama of life.

It is not that Pirandello grew garrulous with age. He believed that the human thing was not merely to live, as the beasts do, but also to see yourself living, to think. Thinking is a function of human life. Whereas in his short stories, as in *Liolà*, he is often content to tell the story from outside, reducing it as much as possible to action, and giving full play to the setting, he obviously regarded the dramatic form as a challenge to show more of the inner life of man, to show man seeing himself, to let characters become roles and speak for themselves. His people "think" a lot, but their thinking is a part of *their* living, not of

Pirandello's speculating or preaching. In such a character as the Father in *Six Characters*, the thought is subordinated to the feeling that produces it. Thought is something he tortures himself with; it is a part of his emotional life.

There is no denying that Pirandello sometimes failed to bring it off. His emotions sometimes dried up, and we are left with brittle ratiocination that remains external to the drama. His standard situations and patterns remained safer ground for him than the territory his ambition reached after. The Preface to *Six Characters* tells us what Pirandello thinks the play is. Despite his assertion that he is describing what he finds there and not merely his intentions, we do not find realized in the work all that is in the description. The very idea that is announced in the play's title has less reality in the work itself than the image of Father and Daughter suffering before the uncomprehending eyes of the actors. The other two plays of the trilogy would peter out in talk if, from time to time, and especially just before the end, Pirandello did not remember his customary scheme and summon his primitive emotional strength.

Insofar as there is a moral conception in the trilogy, it is as much more modest than *Right You Are* as that play, morally speaking, is more modest than *Liolà*. We find neither a smiling mastery of the situation nor even a sad tenacious affection but only *a striving toward the genuine*, starting from the mournful yet horribly justified realization that we live in an age when it is an achievement to have a single genuine feeling. We may have little patience with Delia Morello, the frenetic actress of *Each in His Own Way*, but at least she knows the score and has not given up the game for lost: "in all that is fake, in all that is false, as it grows ever more fake, more false—and you can't get out from under—because by now simplicity itself, as we remake it within us, around us, simplicity seems false—seems? no: *is*—is false, is fake. . . . Nothing is true any more, nothing! And I want to see, I want to hear just one thing, just one solitary thing that is true—TRUE—in me!"

Delia Morello is only a character, yet she voices here what seems to me not only Pirandello's noblest impulse but also the one he was best able to keep within the bounds of art (because it was imposed by experience and not by ambition). *"Non è più vero niente!" Here* is the sense in which nothing is true! What a pity that critics have noticed Pirandello's nihilistic flouting of truth in the philosophic sense and have not noticed that all his work is an effort of heart and mind to find the true in the moral sense, to find at least *"una cosa, almeno una cosa sola che sia vera, vera, in me"*!

3

As with Ibsen, as with Shaw, it is not the many ostentatious ideas that matter but one or two more persistent ideas that lie concealed behind them. This is the place to remember to how large an extent form is meaning. The degrees to which an idea gets expressed in an art—and not merely mentioned—depends on the artistic skill of the writer. For many years even Italian criticism of Pirandello was preoccupied with ideas as mentioned rather than as expressed. It is surprising how little has been said of Pirandello's art.

Even against it. For there are lacunae in his equipment as a playwright, lacunae and deficiencies. A first reading of his forty-four plays leaves us with an impression of monotony. A second reading calls our attention to grave faults in dramatic structure and grave limitations in character portrayal. One of the plays most frequently performed in Italy, *All for the Best,* has a central scene of the rankest ham melodrama. Two that are translated into English and have been highly praised (*Enrico IV* and *The Pleasure of Honesty*) have an expository first act of such cumbersome explanatoriness that one would think the author a plodding mediocrity or a careless hack. Overall structure? Pirandello forces all his full-length plays into the three-act mold whether they really fit it or not. Sometimes he has obvious difficulty (for example, in *Man, Beast, and Virtue*) in making the material spin out. More often one simply remains uncertain about the relation of act to act. How many *real* acts are there in *Six Characters* and *Each in His Own Way*? It is hard to resist Tilgher's conclusion that both plays mark time a good deal. Characters? How few of the personages in Pirandello's plays have an effective existence! Take two or three away during the intermission and no one would miss them afterward. Many of them are uninteresting in themselves and remarkably like most of the others.

Despite its reputation for experimentalism, the dramaturgy of Pirandello stays all too close to the French drawing-room play—we could more flatteringly say to Ibsen were it not precisely the "French" externals of Ibsenism that we find. Within the French frame, Ibsen depicted a classic drama: doom flowers in due season, Crisis is brought to birth by Time. The Ibsenite exposition is admirable, not because the characters give us information without seeming to, but because the exposition is itself drama, furthering, even constituting, the action. Now, as Giacomo Debenedetti has pointed out, Pirandello destroys Time. His events do not grow in Time's womb. They erupt on the instant, arbitrarily; just as his characters do not approach, enter, present themselves, let alone have motivated entrances, but are suddenly there, dropped from the sky. In Paris the six characters were literally lowered on stage in an elevator; it is the quintessence of Pirandellianism. In this sort of drama the Ibsenite exposition is dead wood and breaks in the playwright's hands. For this sort of drama is the aftermath of Ibsenism, drama to end drama.

Not with a whimper, though; with a bang. It is a decadent drama, but it rises at times to greatness and in its full extent (Pirandello's plays being, as Massimo Bontempelli says, a single drama in a hundred acts) is one of the very few profound versions of modern life in histrionic terms. How could an artist so faulty, limited, and, to boot, so ambitious—so unaware, that is, of his faults and limitations—be profound and great?

His strongest weapon is his prose. Its torrential eloquence and pungent force are unique in the whole range of modern drama, and recall the Elizabethans (in contrast with our verse playwrights who imitate the Elizabethans and do not in the least recall them). He gets effects that one would not have thought possible to colloquial prose, thus compelling us to reopen the discussion of poetry and drama, in which it has always been assumed that prose was a limitation.

Although it is not clear that the same feats could be performed in any language but Italian, Pirandello exploited the special resources of that marvelous tongue. The credit cannot all be given to the Italian tradition. Italian critics have themselves borne witness to the originality of Pirandello's style:

> ... always extremely simple (the most naked and economic, the farthest removed from literary "equilibrium," the most truly "spoken" ever heard on our stage), the language of these plays is agile, astute, mobile, full of sap, bursting with inner vitality; the dialogue, restrained, exact, with no ornamental appendages, the images immediate and germane, bends itself wonderfully to follow the sinuosities of psychological processes.*

Thus Tilgher. Debenedetti speaks of the obsessive Pirandellian rhythm as "recitative":

> ... unremitting, throwing itself ever forward toward the same cadence, always the same movement, having only its own anxiety to keep it from monotony. Broken, and angry at its own "openness," it swells outward, it rushes in pursuit, it turns on itself as if to correct itself, as if, with the next touch to recover its balance, contrite because it has never quite

*Adriano Tilgher, *Studi sul teatro contemporaneo* (Rome: Scienze e Lettere, 1928), p. 244.

20

succeeded in explaining itself. And it pounces on the word and devours it almost as if the word were the momentary definition of what should be said but above all because it is the quickest and directest track forward.*

And, consciously or not, Pirandello describes his own achievement in setting forth this notion of dramatic writing:

> . . . so that the characters may leap from the written pages alive and self-propelled, the playwright needs to find the word that will be the action itself spoken, the living word that moves, the immediate expression, having the same nature as the act itself, the unique expression that cannot but be this—that is, appropriate to this given character in this given situation; words, expressions, which are not invented but are born, when the author has identified himself with his creature to the point of feeling it as it feels itself, wishing it as it wishes itself.**

It is clear that Pirandello, theorizing, did not view his prose in isolation from his characters and their activities (the plot). *Liolà, Right You Are,* and his other more successful plays show us that his practice could conform to his theory. Even the more discursive plays are discursive in order that the prose may fully express the nature of men—who, among other things, have brains and think. In Pirandello's dialogue, passion does not commit incest with passion as in D'Annunzio's. It meshes with the rest of life, and especially with thought; and benefits thereby, *even as passion.*

I once had the strange good fortune to see Emma Gramatica in *The Dead City* of D'Annunzio and *The Life I Gave You* of Pirandello on successive evenings. I was surprised to find that Italy does not demand two different styles of acting for the two playwrights. Out of Pirandello has come no "Stanislavsky school" of naturalism and understatement. Although in Italy he was often called "anti-rhetorical," in the theatre of any other country he would be considered rhetorical to a degree. In Pirandello, La Gramatica uses a distinctly elevated style, weaving all the time a sinuous pattern with voice and arms, weaving a web in which the spectator is caught.

In performance Pirandello differs from D'Annunzio not in being less stormy, but in being more effectively so. His anti-rhetoric is a counter-rhetoric to which the performer can bring the traditional technique of the passionate Latin theatre with the happiest results.

---

*Giacomo Debenedetti, *Saggi critici* (Rome: Edizioni del Secolo, 1945), p. 277.
**Op. cit., p. 235.

Sometimes everything about a Pirandello play is weak except the central role. The cause of this is doubtless to be found in the star system of Italian theatre, the lack of good ensembles. The quality of the defect is that, when you have a star before you, the whole play takes on life, and you see that after all it is not a mere essay or speech, but poetry, theatre, and even a drama *sui generis*. Thus it is with La Gramatica's *The Life I Gave You* and Ruggeri's *All for the Best*. You may say that even the protagonist in such a play is hardly a character in the traditional sense. He (or she) is more of an impulse than a person. There is nothing in all the rest of drama resembling such characters. They fall from the sky, they are whirled hither and yon, they cry out in anguish, they sink into the ground. But is not this, in its way, highly dramatic?

At any rate it is poignant theatre, and it conveys a vision of life that cuts below the celebrated ideas. Conversely: the ideas are a superstructure of the vision and of the pain of the vision. And what are they, after all, the ideas that Pirandello calls the pangs of his spirit?

> . . . the deceit of mutual understanding irremediably founded on the empty abstraction of words, the multiple personality of everyone (corresponding to the possibilities of being to be found in each of us), and finally the inherent tragic conflict between life (which is always moving and changing) and form (which fixes it, immutable).*

The common denominator of these intellectual propositions is loneliness, isolation, alienation. As we break the bonds between man and man one after another, and find no other bonds to replace them with—or none that are compatible with our humanity—the sense of separateness in the individual grows from mild melancholy to frantic hysteria. As the invisible walls of our culture crumble, and the visible walls collapse in ever-increasing quantity, a disintegration sets in within the individual personality and lags, not far perhaps, behind the general disintegration. Pirandello cannot claim the dubious privilege of being the only writer to dramatize this situation: all of our profounder spirits have been busy doing so. But he has dramatized it with his own accent and that of his people. His Sicilian intensity and equally Sicilian speculativeness drive him into a sort of metaphysical agony, an arraignment of human life itself. For, if the great human gift is that of words, by what diabolic plan does it happen that words multiply mis-

---

*It is of interest that the "final" formulation here does not seem to reflect an intention of Pirandello's own but a conclusion drawn by one of his critics, Adriano Tilgher, who tells us his language was, in turn, drawn from the work of Georg Simmel. Another curious link between Pirandello and German philosophy.

understanding? The very humanity of man increases his isolation. Such is the idea "behind" one of Pirandello's most famous ideas. "Multiple personality" is a similar instance: Pirandellian man is isolated not only from his fellows but also from himself at other times. Farther than this, isolation cannot go. This is a "nihilistic vision," and no mistake.

It would nowadays be called an existentialist vision: life is absurd; it fills us with nausea and dread and anguish; it gives us the metaphysical shudder; yet, without knowing why, perhaps just because we are *there*, in life, we face it, we fight back, we cry out in pain, in rage, in defiance (if we are Sicilian existentialists), and because all living, all life, is improvisation, we improvise some values. Their Form will last until Living destroys them and we have to improvise some more.

Pirandello's plays grew from his own torment (I overlook for the moment the few precious pages that grew from his joy), but through his genius they came to speak for all the tormented and, potentially, *to* all the tormented—that is, to all men. And they will speak with particular immediacy until the present crisis of mankind—a crisis that trembles, feverishly or ever so gently, through all his plays—is past.

RIGHT YOU ARE

On the face of it, Pirandello's *Right You Are* is the purest instance of "drama of ideas" in the history of the theatre, a veritable exhibition of an idea, the statement of a proposition—that truth is relative and subjective: what seems to me, or you, to be so *is* so. The statement is made in the title *Così è (se vi pare)*, explained by a leading character (Laudisi), and embodied in what the author himself designates a parable. Pirandello seems as single-minded as Aesop, his parable a simple fable, apologue, or exemplum.

If it is rare to find a play so deliberately dedicated to a principle, it is rarer to find one dedicated to a principle that none of us will assent to. What would "assent" mean, anyway? That a certain principle which "seems so" to Pirandello also "seems so" to you or me? What if it did? How can we be sure that it is the same principle as the one he is talking about? Furthermore, if *Right You Are* is true only for Pirandello, why did he write it down? If a man holds the view that views are incommunicable, how can he hope to communicate *that* view? In short, we could not assent to the idea of *Right You Are* even if we would.

Was Pirandello a fool? Had he not taken that elementary lesson in philosophy in which the instructor triumphs over relativism and skepticism by observing that relativism must not become absolute and that the skeptic should be skeptical of skepticism? There is evidence on the point—for example, the following debate:

> A—The world is my idea (*rappresentazione*), and the world is purely ideal (*una idealità*). . . . The world—all that is external to the ego—exists only according to the idea one has of it. I do not see what is; what I see, is.

B—Or is not, my dear fellow. Because you may see badly. That existences outside ours should be little more than appearances without reality outside the ego is supposed by the champions of an idealism which the English call solipsism, and you know that it isn't a new notion—English writers following the philosophy of Berkeley have given it fantastic form. And you will know *Through the Looking Glass*. Suppose, my dear fellow, that I, let us say, do not exist outside your ego except as you see me? This means that your consciousness is one-sided, that you are not conscious of me, that you have no *realization* of me within you (to use an expression of Josiah Royce), that your idea does not live for me.

And it must be so. And here, to turn to art, is our true point of difference. For me the world is not solely ideal, that is, it is not confined to the notion I can form of it: outside me the world exists of itself and alongside me; and in my representation or idea of the world I am to propose to *realize* it as much as I can, creating for myself a consciousness in which it exists—in me as in itself, seeing it as it sees itself, feeling it as it feels itself. And so, nothing symbolic and apparent for me, everything will be real and alive!

Since Pirandello* is not A but B we are forced, I think, to admit that he knew what he was doing and are free to ask: if the relativism is a joke, what is serious in the play? In the midst of an earnest discussion in a Westport home,** someone appealed to the maid who was bringing in the tea things, "What did *you* get out of *Right You Are?*" "I guess it just says, keep your nose out of other folks' business," she replied, thus proving all over again how right Molière was to consult his cook. Such is indeed the simple message not only implicit in the action of the play but explicitly stated by Laudisi at the outset as the serious moral conclusion to the frivolous philosophical argument. "Respect what other people see and touch even if it's the opposite of what you see and touch." The reader should go on to ask, as the actor must, not only what Laudisi says but what he does. For more than two acts he tries to discourage people from interfering with the lives of others. In the third act he decides that talk is useless, but his goal is unchanged: he hopes that a *coup de théâtre* may succeed where reason failed—succeed in demonstrating the wickedness and futility of interference.

Pirandello once said he wanted the play to indicate the triumph of the imagination over mere facts, but the imagination he shows us is

*Writing in the weekly journal *Il Marzocco*, March 7, 1897, in reply to Ugo Ojetti (A), *Il Marzocco*, February 28, 1897.

**The present essay was written shortly after I had directed two productions of the play: one at the Brattle Theatre, Cambridge, the other at the Westport Country Playhouse.

not a philosophical or literary power of imagining what is not, it is insight into what is, insight by means of sympathy, it is compassion, it is love. While the ostensible principle of his play is an unacceptable metaphysic, the real principle is: love your neighbor. To realize how far truth is subjective is to realize that one must respect the subject. Pirandello is defending the person against the dehumanizing influence of society. His special care is for the sanctity of the intimate affections, the right to possess your soul in peace and privacy. These ideas are as old as *Antigone* but have become more relevant than ever with the rise of the police state. And it is not just fanatics who are open to attack. "Many of our best friends" have for years been boosting the public interest and the objective fact above the private interest and subjective fact. The inner life of man has been neglected and mocked, without any perceptible public gain.

The seemingly cryptic figure of the veiled lady in *Right You Are* is perhaps the simplest expression of indignation at this neglect in modern literature. She is the inner sanctum, the holy of holies. Her life being love, she has achieved complete self-sacrifice, she has no identity; she exists only in relationship, she is wife to the husband, daughter to the mother; she is what the husband thinks she is, she is what the mother thinks she is, she is what *you* think she is. On the literal plane, all this is absurd, of course, yet hardly more so than the rest of the play. It is all—to quote Pirandello's own perfect characterization—*una gran diavoleria*, a big joke, a piece of deviltry.

Now under what circumstances does a man champion a philosophy he knows to be fallacious? When he wants to enjoy himself and throw ideas about like colored balls. "You're simply being paradoxical," we say to a friend who champions an error with gusto. But the truth is *not* simple. Part of it is that he has been enjoying the comedy of intellect. Another part is that by stating an error he wants to make you more aware of the truth. Laudisi is not quite a devil's advocate. His method is more like the inverse of a *reductio ad absurdum*: he doesn't take plausible premises and prove that they lead to disastrous consequences, he takes implausible premises and derives very desirable consequences from them. We have seen how he derives from his "absolute relativism" the principle of the golden rule. It is also important to see the totality of Laudisi's speeches in the context of other characters' speeches. Laudisi constitutes a sort of frame for the picture or—more correctly perhaps—the spectacles we see the picture through.

Once the "deviltry" of the play is conceded, even its final leap into the realm of symbol seems fully justified. The audience may be cheated of the answer it is waiting for, but it accepts the *image* of the veiled lady unquestioningly. At that point, in performance, there is usually a gasp of astonishment signaling to the actors that the bullet has shot home. And nothing could better illustrate what this play is like than the fact that its climax is an image. If our first discovery is that the idea of the play is not "truth is relative" but "love your neighbor," our second is that *Right You Are* is not, in any narrow sense, a "drama of ideas" at all. To convince himself he has ideas, Pirandello had to redefine the term. "An artist's 'ideas,'" he wrote in his essay on humor, "are not abstract ideas but feelings, sentiments, which become the center of his inner life, take hold of his spirit, shake it, and, by shaking it, create a body of images." *Six Characters in Search of an Author* may have started in Pirandello's mind with an image of Madama Pace's establishment which he took a note of years before. He also tells us that *Right You Are* was born from "the frightening image" in a dream of "a deep courtyard with no exit."* It is with the imagination, not the ratiocinative faculty, that this courtyard is transformed into the home of the Ponzas (the idea of "no exit" being left to Jean-Paul Sartre).

For Pirandello was, in the fullest professional sense, a playwright. He described one of his plays as "Pinero with a difference," and *Right You Are* is a thriller, almost a who-done-it—with a difference. The audience modestly identifies itself with the foolish busybodies, anxiously asks: Is the girl *her* daughter or *his* second wife?—is led to the one answer and the other in rapid alternation, only to be authoritatively told at the end that the girl is *both* her daughter and his second wife. Luckily, there is another "difference" besides the famous ending—that this thriller contains two other dramas, a tragedy and a comedy.

The tragic action of *Right You Are*, bounded by the arrival and departure of the Ponza-Frola family, derives from an unknown "misfortune": the exposure of three lives to the public gaze reopens the wound; they decide to leave.

The comic action derives from the conflict between Laudisi and the townspeople (principally his own family). The three acts correspond to three stages in this conflict. In the first, the "crowd"—in effect a chorus—investigates the lives of the unhappy trio to the point where two of them come forward in turn and make confessions. In the second, the crowd has the "great idea" of confronting Ponza and Frola. Up to this point, Laudisi has practiced dissuasion. But when, in the third act, the police commissioner refuses to write a fictitious explanation that will satisfy everyone's curiosity, Laudisi the peacemaker becomes Laudisi the mischief-maker. He caps the *coups de théâtre* of the first two

*See *Almanacco Letterario Bompiani,* 1938.

acts with an even greater one by giving Sirelli the idea of bringing over Signora Ponza. At the end, his point is proved and he is victor.

This comic action is repetitious. Yet, if Acts One and Two of Pirandello's play present the same drama three times, the very fact that unfriendly critics are not bored but irritated suggests a positive process rather than merely the author's inability to think of something else to say. For one thing, it is repetition and *change*—change in speed and change in magnitude. Farce (and this is farce-comedy) is a mechanism very much like many of the weird and whirling vehicles of a fairground. Its favorite trick is acceleration to a climax—which is reached, in Pirandello's play, just before the final meeting of the Ponzas and Signora Frola. In each act, the same drama takes place: the Ponza-Frolas are the actors, the townspeople the audience. But it is a bigger, "louder" drama every time. And the tempo is stepped up. Now, while the repetition that stems from sterility merely bores, positive repetition, especially when accompanied by a crescendo and an accelerando, is dangerously full of life and tends to act directly on the nervous system. In more Dionysian works—say in O'Neill's *Emperor Jones* or Ravel's *Bolero*—this is readily admitted. What we are less ready to see is the manic element in *comic* repetition. The final subtlety of *Right You Are* is that the sad and sinister traits that are overt in the Ponza-Frola story lurk also in the farce that frames it: hysteria and madness are not far below the surface. Manic repetition is of the essence of farce, as any page of Molière's prose will testify. John Gay's Macheath is arrested not once but twice, the second arrest being superfluous by the standards of pre-Brecht modern dramaturgy but integral to the pattern of classic farce-comedy. A farce-comedy consists of concentric circles of repetition: around the inner ring of phrases, the outer ring of incidents.

In taking Laudisi to be a comic character, I do not mean that he should be continuously funny but that such a figure is closer to the tradition of clowning than to that of wise uncles, doctor friends, and ministering psychoanalysts. Tell the actor of this part that Laudisi is a *raisonneur*, and you will get spectacles, an avuncular manner, prosy explanatoriness: the philosophy will ride him, not he it. Laudisi is Harlequin in modern dress, a Harlequin who has invaded the realm of philosophy, and who behaves there as he had behaved elsewhere. All his scenes are gags—from the little episode in which he teaches the Sirellis philosophy, through the mirror scene, the butler scene, and the scene with Signora Cini and Signora Nenni on the couch, all the way to his inventing of a ghost story and actual raising up of a ghost. He is what the Italian theatre calls a *brillante*, and should sparkle. He needs the bounding energy, the diabolical rhythm, that we associate with the tradition of the *commedia dell'arte*. The challenge of the part today is that it needs these things much more than what we usually require of our serious actors: subtlety of characterization. The actor of the role of Laudisi does not have the task of helping the audience to understand a complex person with such and such a life history: he serves, rather, the more technical function of a link between the comic chorus and the tragic trio, and also between the action onstage and the audience. He needs a highly developed technique because he has to turn like lightning from tears to laughter, and in the last act to take the play and lift it into the world of fantasy. He needs a personality of strength as well as charm because his presence has to be felt even when he is silent and still.

From the two groups into which the rest of the cast falls, the play demands two distinct ways of acting. One group must play tragedy with a tempestuousness forgotten on our Anglo-American stage and believed to be somewhat foreign to our temperament. The part of Ponza presents the Stanislavsky-trained actor with a teasing problem: what to do about the motivation of a character whose motivation is a mystery? I suppose such an actor can invent motives out of whole cloth, but a pre-Stanislavsky actor, for whom such questions did not arise, would be in a simpler position: he need not ask why Ponza is nearly fainting, he can just take Pirandello's word for it. Pirandello is pointedly uninterested in the final psychological explanation of Ponza's passion, he is presenting the passion itself. The actor's task is to do likewise—and to do it within the imposed frame of a social type (the white-collar worker). Fernand Ledoux at the Comédie-Française has shown that it can be done. Yet, to be sure, the alarming Latin way in which emotion leaps from pianissimo to fortissimo in so few words presents the non-Latin actor with a problem. In all modern drama there is nothing harder to do—or even to decide *how* to do—than the final meeting and exit of the tragic trio. No less forgotten and just as often considered foreign (usually French) is the style of comedy required from the second group of actors. Here again it is futile to hunt the motive. The actor's attention has to be transferred from individual psychology where nowadays it too often concentrates itself on to the task of cooperation with other actors in a matter of craftsmanship. He must suspend his belief that it is harder and better to act a Chekhov role than that of a Keystone cop. He must not resist Pirandello's method by complaining that the characters are not sufficiently individualized. Who ever said the Keystone cops were not sufficiently individualized? One could praise them for not being *excessively* individualized, though any one of them could always step out of the group and have as much individuality as he needed.

An author who insists on a character's being six feet one and having an I.Q. of 120 may be said to be creating "closed" characters; an author who leaves the actor large leeway is creating open ones. Traditionally, the theatre deals in open characters. The author's points can be made in a dozen different ways—with actors of different physique using different "line-readings," and so forth. The members of Pirandello's chorus are open characters. Each actor can try his own way of making the main point (Agazzi's self-importance, for example), and it is for the director to decide if the attempt is in place. The nine actors concerned can be asked to make a quick study of their parts and come to rehearsal each with a creation—a Daumier portrait, as it were. In rehearsal it is discovered whether these creations work. If and when they begin to do so, they have to be coordinated. Comic characters most commonly run in pairs. Sirelli is a crony of Agazzi, Signora Cini of Signora Sirelli, Signora Nenni of Signora Cini: ideally all these pairs would become comic couples enjoying as easy and active a relationship as comedian and straight man in vaudeville. A part like that of Signora Sirelli, which barely catches the attention of the reader, in a production by a *maître* like Charles Dullin, becomes a Dickensian gem. The richness of the part stems, technically speaking, from the fact that the actress can play three distinct relationships—to her husband (whom she bickers with), to Laudisi (whom she flirts with), to Cini (whom she patronizes).

No particular style should be imposed on the actors or even spoken of. A true style will come, if at all, as the bloom on a fruit that has ripened by natural growth and good gardening. You can no more tell an actor to perform with style than you can tell him to be funny, and stylization is the last refuge of the theatrical charlatan. Artificial speech and gesture that can be imposed by decree are not worth decreeing. Such "artificial" style as we have admired—say, Gielgud in Wilde—is the product not of a decree but of practice.

The nine chorus members of *Right You Are* will bring with them (one hopes) a technique acquired in farce or vaudeville, but they will not at once be permitted to display their antics because this play needs (as what play does not?) a certain air of naturalness. Only thus can the unnatural and macabre elements have their full effect. The primary aim of the acting must be social satire: we are moving in middle-class circles in a provincial town.

Some caricaturists start with an exact likeness. When they later distort and exaggerate, they take their cue from the truth: only a long

31

nose is made longer, only a small eye smaller, a fat man fatter. This principle applies to the chorus characters in *Right You Are* and to the stage design.

I want my designer to give me an actual room belonging to the right time and place—not necessarily the room in every detail, but enough to suggest its solid, corporeal presence. He must not "stylize" the room with playful fancies of his own. (A common mistake of playful designers is to caricature the pictures on the wall. If the point is, for example, that a picture is sentimental, an actual picture, well chosen, would make the point more forcibly. Openly to make the picture ridiculous is to insult the spectator by instructing him how to respond. And of all instructions, "Now laugh!" is the most risky. The quantity of laughter out front is generally in inverse ratio to that on stage.) The stage designer should limit himself to what is strictly necessary.

"What do the characters *do* onstage?" I was asked by a famous actor who was worried at the absence in the script of all allusion to eating, drinking, and smoking, and the various activities which his naturalistic technique would be helpless without. I do not believe the answer is to insert them; they contribute nothing. "Necessary" means "necessary to the play as Pirandello conceived it," a classic comedy, an elemental tragedy, a slender thriller—anything but a piece of genre painting. What do these people do? They gossip. The furniture of gossip is—the chair. It therefore seemed to me in keeping with Pirandello's almost fanatic lean-mindedness to provide the actors with nothing but chairs. Lester Polakov, our designer, wished to fill the stage with monstrous chairs, their backs five or six feet high, so that the actors would spend the evening threading their way through a forest of furniture. The high backs would mask so much of the stage that the "blocking" problem would be enormous. But someday the idea should be tried.

In both my productions I raised the curtain on an unpeopled stage with a ring of chairs in the center facing inward to suggest that, the day before, perhaps, a circle of gossips had sat there with their heads together. During the first scene Amalia and Dina are rearranging the chairs in a semicircle, and from here on, the chief physical action was the grouping and regrouping of the chairs; for not only is the whole crowd always gossiping, but the Agazzi family is forever receiving visitors, forever setting the stage for the latest drama and preparing an "auditorium" for the onlookers. It seems apt to give Agazzi and his wife a nervous passion for reordering their room. In addition to satirizing the lower-middle-class love of tidiness and symmetry, it is an external, theatrical equivalent of the inner tension and fever.

In Act One the interviews with Ponza and Frola are presented with the chorus forming a semicircle and the object of their scrutiny occupying the only remaining seat, the piano stool, in the middle. In my mind I had the image of an operating room with watching students. In Act Two Pirandello has written a scene with Laudisi on a couch between two ladies. I decided to make the couch the cynosure of all eyes throughout the act by having Agazzi choose it as the projected meeting place for Ponza and Frola. The actual meeting takes place in the open space in front, the chorus standing behind the couch and semicircle of chairs. Here I had in mind a prize ring with a crowd around— or animals in a cage before a crowd of onlookers. The third act is essentially that old standby among theatrical scenes—a trial scene. The drawing room becomes a sort of court of appeals with the Governor as the chief justice. I brought the one large table of the set out of its corner and placed it at right angles to the audience near stage center. When the Governor sat behind it, flanked by Centuri, Agazzi, and Sirelli, a bench of judges was suggested.

The minor details of my scheme were not the same in the two productions I did, nor would they be the same in any future production. The scheme itself is but one possibility among many. I should be interested in trying, sometime, a more naturalistic treatment. Given a cast of trained clowns, I should also be interested in trying a *less* naturalistic treatment: I can imagine a chorus of comedians jumping up and down like jack-in-the-boxes. Directors understandably stress the tragedy more or the comedy more, according to the special abilities of the actors on hand. A French production I saw was delightful light comedy; my own productions seemed to succeed better on the tragic side. The ideal production that one should aim at would be no compromise or halfway house between tragedy and comedy, drama and farce, but a synthesis of the two. I even think I know how the synthesis might be arrived at, and that is by casting English character actors as the chorus and American realistic actors as Ponza and Frola. I would then keep the whole cast on to do *Six Characters* with the same dual distribution.

I have dwelt on the practicalities of staging because no playwright of our time has had a mind more utterly theatrical. In Appendix A below I discuss the short story which *Right You Are* is based on and find the theatrical version better. An artist of course does not go from one medium to another out of a desire for something better but out of a need for something other. Almost until he wrote *Right You Are* Pirandello said he would not write plays; he feared those misinterpretations at the hands of actors which he later depicted in *Six Characters*. Even after *Right You Are*, he spoke of the plays as a "parenthesis" within the writing of his fiction. If in the latter part of his career he was more a playwright than a story writer it was because the drama—much as he resisted it—corresponded to his vision of life. A poet, whose mind worked in images, he was obsessed, or inspired, by one master-image: that of the theatre. From it he ultimately elaborated his "trilogy of the theatre in the theatre." But already in *Right You Are*, when we see Ponza acting out his drama before his drawing-room audience, we are witnessing "theatre in the theatre."

The notion that "all the world's a stage and all the men and women merely players" is one of the commonplaces of Western civilization. A charming version of it in Italian runs:

> mondo è teatro e l'uomo è marionetta:
> se voi guardate bene nella vita
> ognun vi rappresenta una scenetta

> ("world is theatre, and man is marionette:
> if you take a good look at life,
> everyone in it is playing his little scene")

To say that a man is an actor is normally to condemn him, and the normal procedure of criticism, satire, comedy, is to remove his mask. Pirandello's play *To Clothe the Naked*, following Ibsen's *Wild Duck*, shows the calamitous consequences of so doing. The collective title of his plays is *Maschere nude (Naked Masks)*. People mask the fact that they are masked; Pirandello strips this fact bare and excuses it. The "mask" of his title resembles the *fantasma* (fantasy, ghost) of Laudisi, the *pupo* (puppet) of Ciampa (who is the Laudisi of *Cap and Bells*), the *pagliacetto* (doll) of Diego Cinci (who is the Laudisi of *Each in His Own Way*). Laudisi's mirror speech makes it clear that error consists not in having a ghost, wearing a mask, but in chasing *il fantasma altrui*, the ghosts of other people, the masks of others, in the belief that these are not ghosts and masks but souls and faces. That there *is* a soul, a center of identity, is not questioned by Diego Cinci at least, for he denounces the false mask of one Prestino on the grounds that it does not correspond with what he "really is and can be."

The word *"maschera"* is also used to define the actors of the *commedia dell'arte* who each played one fixed role. The critic who said Pirandello was not interested in characters but in *maschere* probably meant pretty much what people mean when they damn an author for creating "types," not "individuals": types are assumed to be characters of contemptible cardboard, mere snap judgments on social groups. The roles of the *commedia* are a great deal more. They offer as fair a field to the psychologist as any of the modern typologies, and like the latter they represent a delving below both individual and social distinctions for the very elements of our humanity. Now, several of Pirandello's critics (first among them Massimo Bontempelli, I believe) have noticed the elemental quality in his Ponzas and Frolas and have recorded their impression that the Maestro has rendered human nature in its raw and general state prior to individuation. This being so, one is tempted to take the *maschere* in the phrase *"maschere nude"* to mean human archetypes, human beings stripped of the accretions of civilization. If this isn't what Pirandello meant, it is what he ought to have meant. He had every right to claim that he dealt in such archetypes—if only, by the nature of the case, gropingly, by intuition. And the chief function of the theatre in Pirandello's life was that it helped him to do so.

FROM THE LIFE OF THE DRAMA
(TWO EXCERPTS)

1

If the word we associate with Shaw is "ideas," the word we associate with Luigi Pirandello is "cerebral," for the Italian's reputation is not just for having one notion (that appearance *is* reality), but for harping on it, for being unable to let it alone. This, I presume, is what the word "cerebral" is intended to convey, and to deal with the point one must assume that appearance is *not* reality, since Pirandello appears cerebral and one would like to inquire whether he really is so.

If to be cerebral is to think without feeling, it is not possible for human beings to be wholly cerebral, and the question must be restated thus: Is Pirandello *unduly* cerebral? Is there *too little* feeling in his work? His being unable to let his idea alone suggests the contrary, since obsession is not a "coldly intellectual" factor but a hotly neurological one. Is it people who have got their Pirandello secondhand, through bad critics or bad translations, who think of him as "cerebral"? The first thing any sensitive reader would notice in his work is not an abstractness of thought but a tremor of the nerves. And if we pursue this clue we find that Pirandello, more of an Ibsenite than Shaw ever was, retained Ibsen's image of modern man as neurotic sufferer but in revising it deepened the shade of mental sickness. His starting point is not philosophy but emotional disturbance—and not the *theory* of emotional disturbance, as with so many post-Freudian playwrights, but the concrete fact—in short the emotion, the disturbance.

In all three of the Pirandello plays which have entered the world repertoire, *Six Characters*, *Enrico IV*, and *Right You Are*, the principal characters are in turmoil to the depths of their being. If we do not in every case recognize this at once, it is because in our present-day plays such disturbances are labeled to orientate us, whereas in Pirandello we may never find out just what the trouble is, with or without labeling. In *Right You Are*, he makes it the point of the story that the psychic problems are unsolved—the psychic problems, not just the legal identities. Human nature is to be seen, he is telling us, not as a problem but as a mystery—he would have us look into the troubles of the Ponzas and Frolas with the reverent charity of religion rather than the inquisitive, inquisitorial microscope of medical science. Even so, in the two principal accounts of what has happened—one given by Signora Frola, one by Signor Ponza—case histories are provided of a mental distress that goes all the way to psychosis. One story is of a man who was so unable to bear being deprived of his wife's company that he had to conclude she was dead. The other is of a woman who was so unable to bear her daughter's death that she had to believe that another girl is her daughter, who had never really died. In both cases, the subject is delusion brought on by a trauma of deprivation. Traumas of this kind seem to be at the heart of things for Pirandello, and that is one reason why his work is dramatic. Theatre is shock because life is shock.

How did Pirandello proceed from these traumas to a type of drama the world would call cerebral? It is a question of the kind of significance he extracted from the material. Here Ibsen could not give him the answer. For Ibsen, man was neurotic. This was startling to his early audiences but it did not prevent him from writing a drama that was moral in the old way. For Pirandello, there is only a very special kind of ethics to be had—an ethics of compassion in the face of impossibility. The neurosis of man is seen as bordering upon psychosis and occasionally falling headlong into it. Though man may achieve compassion, he is first and foremost, not a moral being, but a pathological one. Yet pathology holds for Pirandello no clinical interest. Rather, it plunges him into despair about existence itself, a metaphysical anguish.

A schizophrenic is out of touch with us, and we with him. The reality of him is not only complex but somehow not there at all, "gone," lost. Such an unknowability and unreachability constitute for Pirandello the human condition generally. Which is a philosophical proposition; but before it is that, it is the "impression" life made on him, a shocking, agonizing impression. Biographical critics have spoken of Pirandello's psychotic wife, but nothing that might be discovered about the Signora could explain how the Maestro himself came to think her condition was, in a profound sense, that of the human race in general, much less how he could give to such an "unsound proposition" a vibrancy that would find a response in the world audience.

The existential situation is terrifying. How shall one probe its meaning? All that man has at his disposal for such a task is words and thoughts. So Pirandellian man, like other men, resorts to words and thoughts. They go round and round in his brain only to produce another terror, another vertigo. Man's intellect, to which alone he can look for explanations of anything whatever, and to which alone he can turn for an explanation of his own misery, fails him—and so becomes a further, more exasperating source of misery. Thought has assigned to itself the task of finding the reality beneath the appearance. It has failed. We have only the appearances, and must hail them, mockingly, despairingly, as reality. Pirandello's "little philosophy lesson" teaches little philosophy. What it teaches is both more than philosophy and less: terror, misery, despair. Pirandello's is the vision of Matthew Arnold's "Dover Beach"—a spectacle of ignorant armies clashing by night. Arnold speaks in that poem of the tide bringing in the eternal note of sadness:

> Sophocles long ago
> Heard it on the Aegean, and it brought
> Into his mind the turbid ebb and flow
> Of human misery . . .

Pirandello listened to this ebb and flow, and in a time called untragic recaptured the eternal note of sadness, restoring to it the turbulence of ancient tragedy.

2

In literature itself, the classical treatment of this theme of "drama in everyday life" is Pirandello's. He went much further than Erving Goffman [in *The Presentation of Self in Everyday Life*], and spoke, not just of *presenting* oneself, but of *constructing* oneself. That is the positive side of Pirandellian philosophy: Pirandello even bolstered his admiration of Mussolini with the suggestion that the *Duce* had excelled us all in "self-construction." But the source of the whole conception lay less in thought than in experience, and painful experience at that, so that it is the negative side of the philosophy that is active in Pirandello's art. The great question raised in his plays is: Where does fact leave off and fiction begin? What is true, what is only imagined? What is life, what is drama? What is real, what is play-acting? At times an out-and-out skepticism is proposed—Gabriel Marcel calls it the most radical skepticism ever propounded—but, perforce, if Pirandello was to create plots and characters at all, this skepticism had often to be left in abeyance, so that distinctions between, say, sane and insane could retain some objective reference. It is only because the distinctions do still mean something that the paradoxes have a point. Even *Right You Are*, where at the end one is invited, at least in jest, to accept a mystical rejection of elementary logic, depends throughout on the distinction between sane and insane remaining meaningful and even clear-cut.

Still, the ending of *Right You Are* is a paean of praise to role playing, to the theatrical view of life, for what it says is: whatever the veiled lady's lost birth certificate may have had on it, her significant identity is that of daughter to the old lady, wife to the executive secretary. She plays the role each wishes her to play. Everyone would agree that this is most "feminine" of her, and Pirandello is adding that he considers it most human and right. Which is an extension into ethics of George Santayana's merely esthetic defense of role playing. For while Santayana is saying that to take up a role gives us *panache*, Pirandello is saying that it is morally praiseworthy. What passes for our "real" identity is something the veiled lady would only stick to out of false pride. Cordelia in *King Lear* sticks at first to her image of herself as one who does not flatter, and who has cause to be hostile to Father. Later, Cordelia melts, loses this identity, and becomes "as he would desire her," all affection and solicitude: "no cause, no cause." Pirandello's veiled lady, all love and duty, can say: "To myself I am no one."

If willingness to accept the role imposed by another can be a virtue, the determination to impose a role upon another is a vice. It is also based on unsound psychology, and its victims will say so. The most agonized of them is the Father in *Six Characters*, who feels he has been hung on the peg of that single moment when he stood exposed as Lechery Incarnate before his own stepdaughter. But Pirandello's critics have generally overstressed the psychological and epistemological side, and missed the moral side. The radical skepticism does not extend to ethics. Rather, Pirandello has contrived to derive a firm ethics from the very lack of firmness all around. *Just because* all is so uncertain, including our own identities, we need consolation, we need pretexts for affection. These pretexts are the roles we play. The veiled lady is saying: "I don't know what anything is or who anyone is. I don't know who I myself am. The more reason to be willing to be anyone, assume any role, that would ease the pain in one's loved ones." Pain, love: these things are not doubted. Hence the legitimacy of a kind of categorical imperative: play any role that would reduce the pain, en-

large the area of love. Santayana's histrionism is intellectual and san-
guine, Pirandello's emotional and desperate.

Drama and life have so much in common, they can easily get confused. In Pirandello's *Tonight We Improvise,* an actress feels herself disturbed by enacting a death scene: art has invaded life, a little fictional
death has entered into nonfictional life, and caused a tremor, a qualm,
a premonition. Simple! But not without far-reaching implications.
The tremor has not (that we know of) been created in the actress we
see in the theatre. The role of the actress is being played by an actress
who has presumably not felt such a tremor. The paradox is stated even
more forcibly in *Six Characters,* where characters are offset by actors,
and the point is made that actors can never attain to the reality of
characters. In the show we witness, however, the characters are also
played by actors. Hence the thesis of the play is refuted by the performance of the play, unless we assume that the actors are *failing* to play
the characters, in which case the performance is a failure. Since we
cannot believe that Pirandello intended all performances of his play to
be failures, we must abide by the notion of a contradiction between
the play and the idea of the play. This contradiction is not so much re-
solved as validated by Pirandello's view of life: we men can only play
roles, we cannot just be. We can conceive of creatures who just are, but
we cannot be them, we can only enact them. Hence the paradox of the
six characters who just are, yet whose "being" cannot be communicat-
ed to us except through enactment. For us then, the enactment, not
the thing acted, remains the ultimate term. Simulation is the only
thing not simulated. Pretense is the ultimate reality.

In a sense, the possibility of a perfect performance of *Six Characters*
is excluded from the start, for it would be one in which we lose the
sense that the "Six" are acted parts at all. Perhaps at moments we can
and do lose this sense, but we are quick, as a little time passes, to realize
that this could only be because the six roles are so well—acted. We cannot forget for more than a moment that the roles are acted or we take
leave of our senses. Like the man who jumps on stage to save Desde-
mona from Othello, we would leap forward to warn the stepdaughter
that "that man there" is her stepfather. Yet, supposing the "Six" roles
are superbly acted, do we not hasten to say that it is just as if six characters had walked on stage without assistance from Actors' Equity? If
we do, the key words are: *as if.* For only these two small words separate
us from lunacy, and the play from dissolving into chaos. We get Pirandello's idea because it is *not* incarnate. He gives it to us at a remove.
However powerful the illusion, we see it through a glass darkly. One
might call Pirandello the last of the Platonists and say he is showing us

41

the shadows in Plato's cave. For, just as in Plato, it is shadows or nothing, so in Pirandello it is the enactment, the improvisation, the play, or nothing. And whether or not he convinces us of his general view of things, whether indeed, as the years pass, his philosophy as such retains any interest, he has created a living image which can never die—the image of man as actor and of life as the game of role playing, *il giuoco delle parti*.

ENRICO IV

A young man loves a woman and is not loved in return. What is more, he has a rival. In a costumed cavalcade, the rival causes the young man's horse to slip, and the young man falls, faints, and, when he comes to, is the victim of the delusion that he *is* the person whose costume he is wearing: the German Emperor Henry IV. His sister converts a villa into a replica of this Emperor's palace so that the young man can live on as Henry IV undisturbed. After twelve years, however, the delusion wears off. Our man, no longer so young, decides not to let anyone know it and to stay on as Emperor, though sane.

After eight more years, his sister dies. But she had visited him shortly before her death and gained the impression that he might now be curable. She tells her nephew this, and soon after her death he brings a psychiatrist to the villa to see what can be done. The psychiatrist, noticing on the wall portraits of our Emperor and the girl he loved, dating back to the time of the cavalcade, proposes a very precise form of shock treatment. He replaces the canvases by living human beings dressed up like the portraits. They make good likenesses, as one is the woman's own daughter, the other is the "Emperor's" nephew. The Doctor next makes the woman herself dress like the portrait. The idea is that the Emperor will notice that the pictures have come alive, then he will see the older woman, then he will look at himself, and noting in shock the difference between the older couple and the younger will be forced out of his illusion of having remained young, of having remained Henry IV.

The Doctor's plan is of course bound to go wrong, since "Henry IV" has known for eight years that he is not Henry IV. Indeed, everyone else finds this out now from his attendants, to whom he has just re-

43

leased the secret. No sooner has he had an instant to receive the image of the two couples than in rushes everyone to announce the truth and confound confusion. But if the incident cannot have the effect on Henry that the Doctor intended, it does have an effect, and the Doctor's first impression is that it has reactivated the insanity, for Henry seems to accept the younger woman as the elder one, and later on tries to define the whole new situation in terms of this illusion, finally taking the girl in his arms. Her mother's lover—Henry's old rival—protests on the grounds that Henry is sane and able to control himself. "Sane, am I?" says Henry, and kills him on the spot.

That is the story of Luigi Pirandello's *Enrico IV*, and there is a temptation to think of the play as just these incidents with a good many little philosophical essays added. Some of the translations read that way, and Pirandello himself must bear the responsibility for some bad storytelling. The exposition is heavy and overcrowded, as maybe Pirandello realized when he wrote the stage direction that instructs the actors to play it vivaciously. Even the climactic scene of the play is badly articulated, for it is not just that Henry hasn't time to take in what is happening over the portraits—the audience hasn't time either.

Confusion here is presented confusingly, as indeed it is in the whole parallel between the modern young man and the Emperor Henry. One could wish that this Emperor were a man some conceivable audience would know about, so that they could recognize any parallels without effort or, failing this, that the story of the Emperor were so simple that the dramatist could put it across along with his modern plot. The very linking of the two stories certainly makes us assume a point-for-point parallel, but this expectation is disappointed, and bafflement results when, for example, while we see only two women on stage (Matilda, Frida) we are asked to imagine four in the life of the Emperor (Matilda, Agnes, Adelaide, Bertha). Nor—to follow through with the same example—do the modern pair always represent the same two medieval ladies. While one medieval figure (Matilda of Tuscany) is represented by both modern women, one of the modern women (Countess Matilda) represents two medieval women (Matilda of Tuscany, Duchess Adelaide). Some Pirandellians may wish to argue that this is the complexity of deliberate legerdemain and is meant to be bewildering, but others may be permitted to wonder how they can be expected to know this. If one is bewildered as to what is going on, must one not also be bewildered as to the author's intentions?

The question with a work of art that is notably obscure is whether the first puzzling acquaintance one had with it afforded such a premium of pleasure that one wishes to come back for more. In the case of

Enrico IV there can surely be little doubt. At first encounter, it is hard to get the facts straight—and therefore impossible to get the meaning straight—but there is no doubt of the powerful impression made by the principal images, speeches, and scenes. The general scheme is itself very striking for anyone with the slightest predilection for Gothic fiction, and there are moments of exquisite theatrical poetry—such as the moment in which Henry dictates his life story to Giovanni—which make their mark even before we ask questions about the main drift.

When we do come to these questions, the first question of all is inevitably: what about this German Emperor? Why did it have to be him? I thought I might find some clues when I found mentioned by Benjamin Crémieux the titles of the books Pirandello had consulted on the subject: Johannes Voigt's life of Pope Gregory VII and Wilhelm Oncken's *Allgemeine Geschichte*. But I did not find much in these that seemed more to the purpose than an encyclopedia article on the subject unless it was two pictures—of the Abbey of Cluny and the palace at Goslar, respectively. Pirandello worked with the elementary facts of Henry's life as they might be related by any history teacher. Because Henry came to the throne as a mere child, his mother, Agnes, acted as Regent. She came under suspicion of adultery with the Bishop of Augsburg and had to be removed. To this bit of pure history Pirandello adds the fiction that the accusation of adultery was brought by an ecclesiastical friend of the Vatican's: Peter Damiani. Aside from this, all that is filled in of Henry's earlier life is that he had trouble keeping his German barons and ecclesiastics in line. Pirandello, like other people, is mainly interested in what happened when Henry was twenty-six: his archenemy, the Pope, brought him literally to his knees and he knelt in the snow at Canossa hoping that the Pope would give him an audience. His wife, the Empress Bertha, knelt with him, and Bertha's mother, Duchess Adelaide, went with the Abbot of Cluny, another friendly witness, to plead with the Pope and the latter's ally, Countess Matilda of Tuscany.

Here Pirandello adds something of more significance than the involvement of Peter Damiani. "I wanted," he has been quoted as saying, "a situation where a historical personage was in love with a woman who was his enemy." Not finding what he wanted, he created it. Matilda of Tuscany was indeed Henry IV's enemy, but no historian records that he loved her. Pirandello invents this motif, and lets us know it in the play itself by having Landolf remark that Henry secretly loves Matilda even though the historians say nothing about it. It is only through his own Matilda that Pirandello's nameless young protagonist comes to the Emperor Henry IV in the first place. The modern Matilda had already picked her medieval namesake as her role in the masquerade, and that is what gave her young man the idea of being Henry:

> I said I'd like to be Countess Matilda of Tuscany. . . . I just heard him saying, "Then I'll be at your feet at Canossa. . . ." I now understood why he wanted to be next to me in the cavalcade as the Emperor . . . because I'd chosen to represent his implacable enemy.

And because he secretly loved her. What the nameless young man finds in history besides a name and the status of an emperor is a relationship of love/hate.

Pirandello's Emperor seems most of the time stuck in his twenty-sixth year (1077), but he has some power to bob about in his private time machine, and is particularly concerned with the years 1076 and 1080. In 1076 at Tribur the German princes had proposed to depose Henry. His famous gesture at Canossa turns out on further scrutiny not to be a sincere and definitive submission before Papal authority but a sly man's effort to head off the prospect of facing his accusers. By 1080 Henry's position had been strengthened to the point where it was not *his* throne that was in danger but the Pope's own. This was an Emperor who, when the Pope was not to his liking, would set up another: the Henry of Pirandello's play prophesies that at Brixen he will declare Pope Gregory deposed. That the historical Emperor outlived by many years both Canossa and Brixen is acknowledged by Pirandello only in the statement that Henry's life contained the material for many tragedies.

It would be a mistake to pursue the historical Henry past the point where Pirandello takes leave of him, or to hunt for more parallels than the play immediately suggests to anyone who knows the historical outline, for beyond this point history will become the play's rival and a victorious rival at that. By putting into the play itself the few historical facts he needs, the author is declaring the other facts off limits. After all, drawing upon some very suggestive incidents and relationships, he has created a plot and characters that are his own and not at all medieval. We perhaps need to brush aside the Gothic trappings altogether for a minute or two if we are to glimpse his characters as they are.

Pirandello is an Ibsenite dramatist. I have suggested above that for Ibsen man is neurotic but that for Pirandello man is even more deeply neurotic, is indeed never far enough from psychosis to be out of danger of falling into it. Has it been noticed how very far gone are all three of the main characters in *Enrico IV*? Pirandello's full awareness of what he was doing in this respect could be illustrated by the stage directions in which some of the characters—Dr. Genoni for instance—are first introduced. But stage directions stand outside the drama proper, and the dialogue itself is rich enough in evidence. Matilda's character, for instance, is defined in the following passage from Act One:

COUNTESS. . . . I *was* natural in those days. . . .

BARON. You see: she couldn't abide him!

COUNTESS. That's not true! I didn't even dislike him. Just the opposite! But with me, if a man wants to be taken seriously—

BARON. —he gives the clearest proof of his stupidity!

COUNTESS. Don't judge others by yourself, Baron. *He* wasn't stupid.

BARON. But then *I* never asked you to take me seriously—

COUNTESS. Don't I know it! But with him it was no joke. My dear Doctor, a woman has a sad life, a silly life. And some time or other it's her lot to see a man's eyes fixed upon her, steady and intense and full of—shall we say?—the promise of enduring sentiment? (*She bursts into a harsh laugh.*) What could be funnier? If only men could see their looks of enduring sentiment!—I've laughed at them. More at *that* time than any other.—And let me tell you something: I can still laugh at them, after more than twenty years.—When I laughed like that at *him*, it was partly from fear, though. Perhaps one could have believed a promise in *those* eyes. It would've been dangerous, that's all.

DOCTOR.—Why dangerous?

COUNTESS (*with levity*). Because he wasn't like the others. And because I too am . . . I can't deny it . . . I'm a little . . . intolerant, that's the word. I don't like stuffiness, I don't like people who take life hard.—Anyway, I was too young at that time, you understand? And I was a woman: I couldn't help champing at the bit.—It would have needed courage, and I didn't have any.—So *I* laughed at him too. With remorse. With real self-hatred. . . .

The same conversation gives us all we need to know of the protagonist before he appears. People laughed at him behind his back:

DOCTOR. Ahem, yes, um . . . he was already rather strange . . . exalted, as it were—if I've been following you properly?

BARON. Yes, but after a very curious fashion, Doctor . . . he was damned cold-blooded about it—

COUNTESS. Cold-blooded? What nonsense! This is how it was, Doctor. He was a little strange, it's true: that was because there was so much life in him. It made him—eccentric.

BARON. . . . He was often genuinely exalted. But I could swear, Doctor: he was looking at himself, looking at his own exaltation. And I believe the same is true of every move he made, however spontaneous: he *saw* it. I'll say more: I'm certain it was this that made him suffer.

47

At times he had the funniest fits of rage against himself . . . the lu-
cidity that came from acting all the time . . . being another man . . .
shattered, yes, shattered at a single blow, the ties that bound him to
his feelings. And these feelings seemed—well, not exactly a pretense,
no, they were sincere—but he felt he must give them an intellectual
status, an intellectual form of expression—to make up for his lack of
warmth and spontaneity—so he improvised, exaggerated, let himself
go, that's about it, to deafen his own ears, to keep his eyes from seeing himself. He seemed fickle, silly, and sometimes . . . yes, ridiculous, let's face it.

Now drama is not made up of character sketches, nor even of characters set side by side: character is rendered by relationships, and relationships are defined in happenings. The happenings in Pirandello are
not only collisions (which would be true of much other drama), they
are traumatic collisions. His plays hinge on scenes that have the quality of haunting fantasies, like the "primal scene" of psychoanalysis. *Enrico IV* is built upon several traumatic moments. The moment when
the protagonist fell from his horse comes first to mind, but of equal
weight is the moment, twelve years later, when he woke up to know he
was not the Emperor. Then there is the moment, eight years after that,
which is the occasion of the action presented on stage, the moment
when the other actors in the original drama dare to return to it after
two decades: such is Act One. The play moves on to two further traumatic moments: the moment when the planned trauma does not take
place, but another one does, as the nameless hero sees the living portraits and the crowd rushes in to say he is sane; and, secondly, the moment in which "Henry" murders Belcredi.

How many readers will notice that the foregoing list omits the most
important trauma of them all? I omitted it involuntarily by a kind of
"Freudian" forgetting that somehow belongs.

> COUNTESS. . . . A woman has a sad life, a silly life. And some time or
> other it's her lot to see a man's eyes fixed upon her, steady and in-
> tense and full of—shall we say?—the promise of enduring senti-
> ment? . . .

We know she is describing the unnamed one's love for her. He picks up
the thread at the very climax of his eloquence in Act Two.

> Woe betide you if, like me, you are swallowed up by a thought that will
> really drive you mad. You are with another human being, you're at
> their side, you look into their eyes—how well I remember doing it that
> day!—and you might as well be a beggar before some door you will nev-
> er pass through!

In comparison with a murder, or a fall from a horse, the incident is small, but I call it the most important trauma of them all because without it the other traumas either would not have occurred or would have much less significance. At the heart of this Gothic quasi history, this Germanic quasi-philosophical treatise, is a Sicilian melodrama—or opera libretto, if you will—love, jealousy, and revenge. The culmination of such a melodrama is the death of the rival, and the first stage along the violent road to this destination was reached when the rival tripped the hero's horse. Pirandello's plays are variants on such patterns, and Pirandello is giving this particular pattern a new center when he brings the eyes of hero and heroine together, not in the expected exchange of love, but in the unexpected failure to exchange anything. The woman's eyes are a door the man will never pass through. This incident, this situation, undercuts the melodrama because, now, victory over one's rival is fruitless: love is not to be had anyhow. In this way, melodrama becomes drama "of the absurd," becomes "grotesque" in the sense Jan Kott uses the term when he states that in a grotesque work "both alternatives of the choice imposed are absurd, irrelevant, or compromising."

Kott is concerned not with melodrama but with tragedy. "What once was tragedy," he says, "today is grotesque." This too is a thesis which *Enrico IV* exemplifies. The play has been described as Pirandello's one real tragedy, and in some Italian editions it is subtitled *Una Tragedia*. It is certainly Pirandello's *Hamlet*. Belcredi is its Claudius, Countess Matilda its Gertrude, Frida its Ophelia. And Hamlet's antic disposition has spread itself over the whole life of the Pirandellian protagonist.

There is *talk* of tragedy in the play. For if the nameless one has chosen to be Henry IV because the latter is the enemy of Matilda of Tuscany, he has chosen him equally because he was the *tragic* emperor, whose life indeed contained "material for many tragedies." (Henry IV is called *il tragico imperatore* in Pirandello's *Rhenish Elegies*.) His aim in life is nothing less than to attain to tragic seriousness, as he makes quite explicit in the speech about the priest who returns to his priestliness from the truancy of a frivolous dream. "Back into his eyes came the same seriousness that you have seen in mine, for Irish priests defend the seriousness of their Catholic faith with the same zeal I felt for the sacred rights of hereditary monarchy."

The protagonist insists on tragedy; the author does not. The protagonist is a character in search of the tragic poet: such is Pirandello's subject, which therefore comes out absurd, grotesque, tragicomic. "Comic" is the conventional opposite of "tragic," even as joking is the usual opposite of seriousness. In Pirandello's play, the protagonist's wish to be serious, to be taken seriously, stems from a feeling that he is *not* serious, that people do not take him seriously. This we are told at the outset, where Matilda speaks of "all the fools who made fun of him," after which Pirandello never lets the theme go. Is Enrico ridiculous, or isn't he? Are people laughing at him or aren't they? Are his actions jokes and jests or aren't they? The words "joke" (*scherzo*) and "jest" (*burla*) are reiterated obsessively, and always in connection with making a joke or jest of something that should *not* be joked or jested about. Matilda is, in this respect, the agent of the action, since she does, or has done, the laughing. And she has turned from the man she laughed at in fear to the man she laughs at in scorn. *Everything that happens in the whole bizarre series of events is a joke,* bad or good. The idea of the cavalcade was a joke. The tripping of the horse was a practical joke of Belcredi's. The original joke of the masquerade is perpetuated by the re-creation of the Goslar palace in an Umbrian villa. The action we see on stage is meant seriously by its instigators but is turned into a joke by others. The exposition is intended as farce (even if it does not quite work out that way). Genoni is a doctor out of Molière or Ben Jonson. His grand design is closer to *commedia dell'arte* than to the clinic, and Belcredi is there to make us aware of this. A high point in the action is reached when the nameless one reveals to the attendants that he is not mad. The conclusion they draw is that his life in the villa has been a jest. This interpretation produces "Henry's" first great burst of rage. His second, which ends the play, grows out of an act-long quarrel between Belcredi and himself about this matter of joking. "The whole thing was a joke . . . he put on an act so he could have a good laugh behind your back . . . let's have done with this perpetual jesting!" The attendants have told Belcredi the madness was a jest. Belcredi calls the masquerade a joke, and the nameless one counters with: "it wasn't such a joke to me as you think."

The ending of the play, which perhaps seems arbitrary when we detach it from the thematic structure, grows organically enough out of the perpetual torturesome question: Is anything more than a jest at stake? The effect of the Doctor's shock treatment is to make the nameless one review the whole situation not in philosophic calm but in the frenzy induced by the crisis. What he comes back to again and again is the danger of being ridiculous—of his tragedy being reduced to a comedy. Should he, now that he is cured, go out of doors and be a modern man? "To have everyone secretly pointing at me and whispering, Emperor Henry?" When Matilda says, "Who could even conceive of such a thing? An accident is an accident," the nameless one reaches back to the basic fact and premise of the whole fable: "They all said I was mad—even before—all of them!" To this Belcredi retorts, "That was only a joke!" He thinks the retort will make matters better: it makes them much worse since the question of frivolity is even more crucial than that of sanity. The nameless one angrily shows his gray hair. Is that a joke? Then he comes out with the true story of how his horse was tripped. "That must have been a joke too!" Then he defines his own general position as a transcendence of jokes: "not a jest, no, a reality." "And one walks around—a tragic character." Thence to the main situation of the last act, the re-creation of the young Matilda in her daughter Frida. "To me it could hardly be the joke they intended, it could only be this terrible prodigy: a dream come alive." He embraces the living dream. Belcredi cannot believe he is "serious" and protests. Not serious? Not serious? How can the jealous rival prove he is not joking, not play-acting? By using a real sword and producing a real death. In this way the nameless one preserves his image of himself as tragic hero, while Pirandello, by the same stroke, decisively detaches his play from tragedy. For, after all, what our hero has just done *is* crazy, *is* ridiculous, and objectively he has tragic dignity just as little as other lunatics who pose as emperors.

In distinguishing between the protagonist's image of himself and Pirandello's image of him, I am declining to take the play as a *pièce à thèse* in which the hero is the author's mouthpiece. It is true he often gives voice to sentiments concerning illusion and reality which we at once spot as Pirandellian commonplaces. Taken as *pièce à thèse*, *Enrico IV* is very neat indeed. It says that "Henry" was all right till these interlopers came to try and cure him. He was all right both in having recovered from insanity and in having found a solution that is even better than sanity: the conscious acceptance of illusion as a way of life. What the interlopers do bids fair to cancel the solution but "Henry" preserves it and perpetuates it the only way he can. The final murder, thus understood, comes to us simply as a logical conclusion and we respond not with a gasp of horror but with a nod of the head—Q.E.D. Similarly, we have to take the play as wholly abstract: we cannot for a moment take the characters as men and women and ask questions like: What kind of person commits a murder of this kind? What would you make of a murder like this if it happened in your own family circle?

Such an approach overlooks what Pirandello has himself put into this play. Though his "Henry" woos and perhaps wins us with his magnificent speeches about illusion and reality, the action of the play does not confirm Henry's theories (i.e., his hopes). What does he actually conclude when he finds himself sane? That so long as the others do not *know* him to be sane, they will provide him with an unusual privilege: that of living in a dream world for the fun of it with the support of all one's friends. Normally one's friends exact a price: they require that one be really insane. So Henry's opportunity was unique! One's first impulse is to call what he is doing "Living the illusion but being the only one to see through it." But of course the others see through it too. They only don't know that he does. So what we have is a compact based on a misunderstanding created by a benevolent deception. This compact generates a certain amount of good. It would therefore be bad to threaten it. But, on the other hand, it has not produced a little Utopia, not even an ideal state of affairs for a single man. For "Henry's" scheme, in its highest flights, does not work. He would like to insert himself into the eleventh century and simply "be." The pleasure of history, as he expounds it, is to be Henry IV forever. But he is confused as to just how to achieve this. It could mean that he is forever Henry IV at the moment of Canossa, in which case he will always be twenty-six years old. Or it could mean that he is free to move up and down the whole life of Henry IV, enjoying the fact that what happens is already settled and one need not live in uncertainty. The confusion here, clearly enough rendered by Pirandello, is not that of a theory but of a man—a madman.

On whose authority do we have it that the nameless one was ever cured? Only his own. But will not many a psychotic claim to be well? It is perhaps curious how easily readers of Pirandello accept Henry's own claims. They could say that, in a degree, Henry offers proof that what he says is true: *He* knows he isn't really a German Emperor, and *we* know he isn't really a German Emperor. But is merely the absence of this delusion a proof of sanity? At this point we may well bog down in semantic difficulties. What *is* sanity? It is Pirandello himself, however, who makes us unaware of this danger. His punning on the word makes us ask finally if *sanity* is any more *sane* than *insanity*. But without looking for a solution of the semantic problem, can we not go on to say that, sane or insane, the protagonist of *Enrico IV* is presented as a deeply disturbed person? And by "presented" we mean "presented to our eyes and ears"; we are not talking of his mental health eight years earlier. In fact, I have already quoted the passages in which it is heavily underlined that "Henry" had been conspicuously abnormal from the beginning. Is it not perverse, then, to see the murder he commits as a merely symbolic affair? Murder is a serious business, committed in massive rage that has had much time and much reason to accumulate: only thus, generally speaking, can we find it credible. But just such factors are present in the play. The murder (*pace* the semanticists) itself seems crazy. And the rhythm of the action seems to derive from the reactivization of the nameless one's trouble through the incidents we witness. This reactivization is prepared dramatically as early as Act One. What is going on inside "Henry" in that act can scarcely be judged on first reading or seeing: there are too many surprises to take in and one doesn't know what to look for. But then first acts in general are to be appreciated at *second* reading. At such a second reading this first act hardly gives the impression of a sane "Henry," even if we make allowance for deliberate whimsy and playfulness on his part.

Let anyone who thinks the nameless one has constructed a foolproof illusion consider what its major premise is: that time can be stopped. "Henry" *has* stopped time to the extent that he can stay in the eleventh century and never need to jump to the twentieth. Even this, however, he achieved only when he actually thought he was the Emperor: when the twelve years were up he knew exactly which century he was in. As to stopping time in the more vital sense that his own body should stay the same age, the nameless one has no illusions: his gray hairs tell him all. And in exploring Pirandello's handling of the point we learn not only that *he* had no illusions either, but that he handled the matter dialectically and brought it to a conclusion not only different from popular "Pirandellianism" but diametrically opposite to it. His hero tried to go on being the twenty-six-year-old German Emperor, yet not only could not build himself a heaven in fantasy, but longed for the other life, the twentieth-century one, that he was missing. Pirandello audaciously places Henry's confession of this at the end of Act One. Is it contradicted by the fact that when later the doors are opened, and the nameless one could go out in the modern world, he refuses? It is; but the contradiction is that of his character and of a universal human situation. True, he has an alibi: it is too late. But when would it not have been too late? Is this a melodrama in which a healthy Innocent has been deprived of his rights by the Villainous Belcredi? At some moments, *he* can think so; but not at all. And at no moment can *we* think so. This is a story of a life not lived in a world of people incapable of living.

Has the fantasy, then, no positive content at all? It has. Here again the thinking is two-sided and dialectical. "Henry" has found himself a *modus vivendi,* and it is true that the visit of the Doctor and the others destroys this (until he builds it up again on another foundation), but the *modus vivendi* was itself imperfect, flawed, full of tragicomic conflict caused by two factors already suggested: the impossibility of the main endeavor (stopping time) and, secondly, the precariousness of the structure of deception and misunderstanding (sooner or later the happy accidents must have an end). It follows that Pirandello's own vision—as distinct from that of some of his Pirandellian spokesmen—is not just of illusion within illusion: there are non-illusions here. Or, stating this differently, illusions are finally only illusions, and one sees through them. It is, on the other hand, no illusion that the nameless one's hair turned gray; or that Belcredi, at the end, is dead as a doornail.

The illusions which many harbor about Pirandello's illusionism come perhaps from assuming that his plays are *about* the philosophy, an assumption it was easy to make when the philosophy was novel and shocking. What is such a play as *Enrico IV* really about? What is at the center of Pirandello's interest, and hence of his play? Necessarily, since he is a major playwright, not a philosopher, what is at the center will not be opinion as such but experience. What he gives us is in fact the *experience* of a man with Pirandellian *opinions*, a man who has applied himself to the Pirandellian task of "constructing himself." That was the meaning of his "play-acting" even in advance of the masquerade. That was the meaning of the masquerade itself and, involuntarily, of the insanity afterward. The point is that "Henry" *always failed*. We even learn in the last act that while he was Emperor (presumably in the "insane period") he noticed his hair turning gray—noticed, that is, that the whole scheme had broken down. In the later phase in which we encounter him on stage he claims to find a solution in *being aware* that one is only an actor in a masquerade, which is preferable, he says, to being such an actor without knowing it. But the play does not show that it really makes much difference whether one is aware of such things or not. Certainly, the four attendants don't "buy" the idea. The one happy human moment of the play, that between "Henry" and Giovanni, is created, significantly enough, by a misunderstanding: Giovanni thinks "Henry" is still mad. And the last act would seem to say that sooner or later any construct is destroyed by life itself.

If the play as a whole embodies a philosophy, that philosophy is pessimistic and materialist, whereas "Henry" is an optimist and idealist. Just think how this *Hamlet*-parody differs from *Hamlet* in its last act. Claudius *has* to be killed: heaven itself has said so. And if there is foul play in the killing, Claudius himself is responsible. In *Enrico*, the murder is itself foul play, a vicious and shabby act: a swordsman stabs an unarmed man in the belly. Was Pirandello remembering Eilert Løvborg's failure to shoot himself in the head? At all events, the belly is the least heroic of close-range targets. The thought makes Henry's presumed heroic image of himself all the more fantastic. The note that is struck here is of course the modern one. This is not tragedy, a heroic genre, but post-Dostoyevski psychological drama showing the decline and fall of a man through mental sickness to crime.

Are Pirandello's plays more about reality and illusion than they are about love and absence of love? The search for truth is generally conducted by the trivial and bad people in them, while the more serious people seek love. It may be said that the latter often declare love to be unattainable. But what relief there is in seeming to discover the undiscoverability of what one is all the time seeking! Yet love is not inherently impossible to the people Pirandello presents. It has only *become* impossible—and for psychological, not metaphysical, reasons. The whole of *Enrico IV* lies in germ in Belcredi's original description of the nameless one (already quoted) as a man suffering from a strange exaltation and always watching his own exalted state, a sufferer who had fits of rage against himself, an actor who, through acting so much, lost touch with himself, a man who lacked spontaneous warmth, and who, to make up for this, improvised and play-acted to the point of the ridiculous. The same part of Act One lets us see that self-hatred and self-abasement are a sort of family neurosis in which all three main characters are sunk. Here surely we find Pirandello's ultimate reason for lighting on the Canossa story: the Emperor Henry IV has fixed only one thing in the memory of the world, his act of self-abasement before the Pope. All the more interesting, of course, if this Emperor's gesture proves, upon closer examination, to have had low cunning in it. We then realize all the more vividly that there was no humility in the action: it was ignoble through and through.

"In stories like this," says the Gardener in Giraudoux's *Electra*, "the people won't stop killing and biting each other to tell you the one aim of life is to love." Here, too, is the modern note: love can be all inference, while what is exhibited is lovelessness and hate. So with Pirandello, love is absent; present are self-hatred, self-abasement, self-mockery. The "loss of self" here is not mere absence of self, let alone a mere theory that there *is* no self, it is an assault on the self by the self. At the psychological center of this play is psychic masochism, brilliantly suggested at the outset by the nagging, irritable, sarcastic tone in which Belcredi and Matilda address each other. The nameless one's final assault upon himself takes the form of murder. While from the viewpoint of "Pirandellianism" the murder of Belcredi may seem laudable, within the world created by Pirandello in his play it is but the final culmination of this masochism and is to be construed (like most murders, after all) as the ultimate measure taken by the murderer against himself.

If this sounds grandiose, I would suggest that, on the contrary, the present line of thought permits one to speak more "realistically" (i.e., literal-mindedly) about both the play and its protagonist. It is the story of the orphan whose orphanhood has been compounded by insanity and incarceration. We meet him at a time that is especially unfortunate even for a man of many misfortunes. The sister who had been something of a mother to him has just died. This great loss is duplicated on a more trivial scale by the loss of the servant Tony who had played the role of Bishop of Bremen. While he is suffering intensely from the pains of deprivation (just such pains are responsible for the mental trouble in *Right You Are*, incidentally), the nameless one is arbitrarily confronted with the one woman he has ever loved and the man who stole her from him by the trick which made him a madman. As if these factors would not be enough to produce an explosion, Dr. Genoni then adds his preposterous plot. Genoni's drama did not show the nameless one that he was irretrievably cut off now from Youth as shown in the portraits. It brought to life the portrait of the Loved One and thus seemed to offer the nameless one all he had ever wanted: Matilda when young. At no point is it brought home to us more vividly than here how aware "Henry" has really become of the loss of both Matilda and his youth. Otherwise he would not be so struck by this living image which he knows is not really Matilda. He is not "taken in," but he is overwhelmed with feeling, and, when Belcredi intervenes, the irritability which would be the normal response has reason to be multiplied a hundred-fold in a rage that means murder. Illusions are falling before realities, right and left. And the conclusion is renewed illusion? Not exactly. There will be a pretense of it, that is all: an illusion of illusion. The reality is that the nameless one, already parentless, childless, brotherless before the "play" started, has now lost the Attendants as far as their old roles are concerned, and has reduced himself to an ultimate misery. Not only can he no longer dream of being cut loose from his Emperor, he cannot even live as Emperor either, for the Attendants no longer believe him mad. At the end he is as "cabined, cribbed, confined" as a Beckett character up to the waist in earth or up to the neck in a jar.

SIX CHARACTERS IN SEARCH OF
AN AUTHOR

A man has a wife and a male child. He also has a male secretary. Between the wife and the secretary there arises what the husband considers an understanding of a harmless sort. He wants to help them in some way, but whenever he speaks to them they exchange a significant look that seems to ask how they should receive what he says if they are not to annoy him. But this itself annoys him. He ends up firing the secretary. Then he sends the wife after him. In the wife's view, he fairly throws her into the secretary's arms; and the pair set up house together. The husband, however, does not lose interest in the wife. His continued interest, indeed, though he considers it "pure" (that is: asexual) is a source of embarrassment to the former secretary. When a daughter is born to the lovers the husband is interested in her too—more, perhaps, even, than he had been in the wife. And when she becomes a schoolgirl, he waits for school coming out, then on at least one occasion seeks her out, and gives her a present. The girl does not know who the strange gentleman is. At a certain point the secretary can bear the whole situation no longer, and he takes his family—there are three children by this time—to live somewhere else, out of the stepfather's reach. Subsequently the secretary dies. His family of four is now destitute; they all have to sleep in the same room. And at some point they return to the place where the husband lived. Here the mother gets employment as a kind of seamstress. But her employer's real interest is in employing the daughter, now in her late teens, as a prostitute. The dressmaker's shop is a front for a brothel. One day, the husband, a client of the establishment, presents himself and would have taken the girl in his arms had not the mother suddenly turned up to cry, "But it's my daughter!" After this encounter, the husband takes his wife back into his home, along with his three stepchildren. At the time he is living with his own son, now in his early twenties. This legitimate son is offended by the presence of the three bastards, and wanders from room to room in his father's house, feeling displaced and desolate. The three bastards react to his hostility. The little girl, aged four, falls into the fountain in the garden and is drowned. The other child, a fourteen-year-old boy, witnesses the drowning, fails to offer any assistance, then shoots himself. The mother, who might have been keeping an eye on the young pair, was, instead, following her twenty-two-year-old son around the house, begging for forgiveness. He rushes out into the garden to escape her, and there comes upon his stepbrother just at the moment the latter watches his sister die and kills himself. After this debacle, the older girl rushes away from home. Left behind are father, mother, and son. . . .

I am trying to tell the story of *Sei personaggi in cerca d'autore*, or rather the story of the six characters *in* the play. This is quite hard,* and an analysis of the work might well begin with the reasons *why* it is hard. The first reason is pretty much what it would be with an Ibsen play. It is hard to tell the story of, say, *Ghosts* because it comes out in fragments and the fragments have to be painstakingly fitted together. The Ibsenite has, above all, to be able to take a hint; he even has to have the detective's knack of snapping up bits of evidence and holding them in reserve till he can connect them with something else. However, while Ibsen's fragments come together into a complete and coherent picture, like the pieces of a jigsaw puzzle, Pirandello defies a number of the normal expectations and, by the usual criteria, his picture is incomplete. As to *location*, for instance, which in the drama, at least since Aristotle, has always been considered something to have a clear understanding about. In most plays one knows exactly where everything takes place, and in plays where the location is somewhat abstract, there is a convention to make this abstractness acceptable to its audience. In retelling Pirandello's story just now, however, I paused several times, hoping to insert a phrase indicating where someone had gone or returned to. The husband's house could be in Rome, I suppose, but couldn't it just as easily be anywhere else with a climate favorable to fountains? Could I even say, "returned to the city"? Not even that; because the only clues are a school, a house with a fountain in the garden, and a modiste's shop that is also a brothel; things that exist in small towns and villages

---

*The plot or non-plot is incorrectly summed up not only in handbooks (Burns Mantle, F. K. W. Drury) but by reputable critics such as Joseph Wood Krutch. Indeed my own summary originally contained a bad inaccuracy which Robert Brustein pointed out to me.

as well. It is not, of course, that one insists on naturalism, but that one cannot react without a degree of bafflement to not knowing *under what circumstances* the secretary lived with the wife in city, town, or village; how far away he then took her; where the bedroom in which all four slept was to be found; and so on. But the queries as to *place* only lead to similar queries on other topics, and notably *time*. Here at least Pirandello has marked certain boundaries, notably the ages of the four children. Since the legitimate son is twenty-two, and the eldest bastard is eighteen, it follows that the transfer of the wife from husband to lover occurred about twenty years ago. Yet, in the Pirandellian context, how little this arithmetic means! In Ibsen, doing such arithmetic usually proves well worthwhile, but in *Six Characters* it would never be done at all, except by such an undiscourageable investigator as myself, willing to follow any trail. This trail has proved a false one. In the rare instances where exact notation of the passage of time is going to affect our sense of drama, Pirandello does the arithmetic for us. The reiterated statement that the secretary died "two months ago" tells us that the death marks the beginning of the Action that is this play, just as the father's death marks the beginning of the *Hamlet* action, and the aunt's death the beginning of the action of *Enrico IV*.

Generally, time and space, in the story of the *Six Characters*, are alike rather abstract and are tokens of a pervasive abstractness. *Who is the Father?* The question: What does he do? is no more answered than: Where does he live? To place him, either literally or figuratively, all we can do is remark that his vocabulary marks him as something of an intellectual—a student of Pirandellian philosophy, even—and that his having a secretary and a sizable house (with rooms to wander through and a garden with a fountain in it) marks him as well-to-do. By contrast, wife and secretary are defined as *poor*, the Italian word *"umile"* leaving open whether they were just of humble birth or also humble by nature. Of the elder girl we know that poverty made her a prostitute; and we see that she resents her father. Of the two youngest children we learn little except that their birth was illegitimate. The young man is so withdrawn and silent that we can be told he is a character not fully created because not suited to a play at all: only part of him, as it were, is there. To say the least, then, these are people of no particular background. We can say they are Italians, but our evidence is only that the play is written in Italian. We can say they are bourgeois, yet even for this the evidence is largely negative: in our culture, the bourgeois is the norm, and the speech of this play is normal, except for Madama Pace, who, like lower-class New York City today, has a Spanish accent. Incidentally, only Madama Pace has a name. Does that make her the only character portrayed with particularity? Hardly; her name is a symbolic one. It means peace, and is presumably used ironically: she brings not peace but a pair of scissors.

Plays without what are called individual characters, with characters labeled The Father and the like, are no new thing. They were the usual thing in the Expressionist plays of the second decade of the century, the decade during which the ideas for *Six Characters* came to Pirandello.* Is this an Expressionist play, then? One is certainly encouraged to believe so by the stage direction in which the six are introduced. All, says the author, are to wear masks which

> will help to give the impression of figures constructed by art, each one unchangeably fixed in the expression of its own fundamental sentiment, thus: REMORSE in the case of the Father: REVENGE in the case of the Stepdaughter; DISDAIN in the case of the Son; GRIEF in the case of the Mother, who should have wax tears fixed in the rings under her eyes and on her cheeks, as with the sculpted and painted images of the *mater dolorosa* in church.

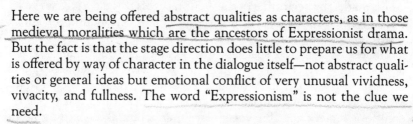

Here we are being offered abstract qualities as characters, as in those medieval moralities which are the ancestors of Expressionist drama. But the fact is that the stage direction does little to prepare us for what is offered by way of character in the dialogue itself—not abstract qualities or general ideas but emotional conflict of very unusual vividness, vivacity, and fullness. The word "Expressionism" is not the clue we need.

---

*The evidence for this is in two short stories, "Tragedy of a Character" (1911) and "Conversations with Characters" (1915), in a letter to his son Stefano dated 1917, and in a passage (undated) from a projected novel-in-the-making cited in the sixth volume of the collected works (1960). This last-named passage is about Madama Pace's establishment, and suggests the possibility that it was with this image that *Six Characters* began—a tempting point in the light of the interpretation of the play offered above. The letter to Stefano is also cited to this extent in the sixth volume of the collected works:

> . . . But I already have my head full of novelties! So many short stories. . . . And a queer thing, so sad, so very sad: *Six Characters in Search of an Author*: novel-in-the-making. Maybe you understand. Six characters, caught in a terrible drama, who visit me to get themselves put into a novel. An obsession. And I don't want to know about it. I tell them it's no use. What do I care about *them*? What do I care about anything? And they show me all their sores. And I send them packing . . . —and in this way finally the novel-in-the-making turns out to be *made*.

Incidentally, in the projected novel-in-the-making, Madama Pace's shop did have a precise location: Rome.

What is? Perhaps the phrase: "dream play." Some of the earliest critics of Pirandello's plays noticed that, in them, "life is a dream." Two features, more than anything else, contributed to this impression: first, the "dreamlike" comings and goings to and from nowhere of Pirandello's people; second, that the author seems haunted, "possessed," by these people. Now the first of these features, appearing by itself, need not signify very much. It is a formal device any author might choose to adopt. It would prove nothing more than that, perhaps, he had read Strindberg. The second feature, however, if further explored, will lead us deep into Pirandello's play, whereupon we shall also learn that, for him, the first feature was not lightly adopted or trivially used.

What is Pirandello possessed *by?* That dramas should present the dynamics of relationship, and not separate individual portraits, is in the nature of the genre. But Pirandello is an extremist in this regard. No one has made do with so few individual traits and details of background while managing to make the contact between people so electric. This kind of drama, one is tempted to say, is ALL relationship and NO character. Six *Non*-Characters in Search of an Author! Or, translating this from negative to positive: In Search of an Author, these relationships—Man/Wife, Father/Daughter, Mother/Son. There can be little doubt what Pirandello is possessed by: elemental family relationships. Our next questions, then, should be: If he has not offered us a cold typicality but has brought relationships to passionate life, how has he done it? If he has not approached these relationships in the accepted, naturalistic way, how *has* he approached them? And now our queries are turning back on themselves, for Pirandello's method has already been touched on, and is that of dreams, not the dreams of the older literary tradition, either, but the actual fantasies of our actual day and night dreaming. And here it would be well to limit the word "phantasy" to the technical sense given it by Freud when he said, "Phantasies are psychical facades constructed to bar the way to . . . memories" of primal scenes.* (Like Freud's translator, I will spell the word with "ph" when this sense is intended.) This may be only one kind of fantasy among many, but it is amazing how close to the principal images and thoughts of *Six Characters* Freud's definition brings us.

In this play we are never far away from primal scenes, and specifically three of them: incest of father with daughter; the child seeing the

*See letter to Fliess dated May 2, 1897, and the accompanying note. Also *The Interpretation of Dreams*, trans. James Strachey (New York: Basic Books, 1955), p. 491.

parents make love; and sibling murder. Each of these scenes is veiled by at least one layer of phantasy. Even the sibling murder, which comes closest to such a scene, is not actually a murder: the boy refrained from preventing a drowning. In the case of the incest, two layers of phantasy at once present themselves. The girl is not a daughter but a stepdaughter, and the love-making does not quite take place. The most thoroughly hidden of the three primal scenes is that of the son seeing his father in the role of lover; and how strong was Pirandello's wish to hide this scene is shown in the fact that he deleted from later editions this passage from the first:

> Hasn't he [it is the Son, speaking of the Father] acted in such a way as to force me to discover what no son should ever discover? That father and mother are alive and are man and woman, for each other, outside the reality we give them. For as soon as this reality is uncovered, our life is no longer tied to that man and that woman except at a single point— one which will only shame them should we see it.

A single point. One touches one's parents at the moment one is conceived. There, for the one and only time, as the parental genitals touch, are all three of us touching. It is the only togetherness life affords. Such is the painfully vivid Pirandellian version of this primal scene. It links the Old Testament shame at the sight of parental nakedness with the Pascalian sense of hopeless isolation in an alien universe. The specific veils the scene wears are also of interest. First, this Son has not discovered *anyone* making love. What he has done is notice the erotic quality in a relationship he did not expect to be erotic. It was not that of his father and mother. It was that of his father and his stepsister. But the suspicion is—and it is not the suspicion of the son alone—that the stepsister is taking the mother's place in bed.

A psychoanalyst, Dr. Charles Kligerman, has made an observation that digs deeper into the plot of *Six Characters* than anything, so far as I know, that purely literary critics have said. It is that we have here not an assortment but a *sequence* of phantasies, each more primitive than the last—each belonging to an earlier phase of our lives than the last. In other words, from adult father/daughter incest there is a retreat to the earlier Oedipal triangle, and then a sudden regression to the primitive sibling rivalry, with wishful phantasy of murder followed by guilty suicide.*

---

*Kligerman, "A Psychoanalytic Study of Pirandello's *Six Characters in Search of an Author*," *Journal of the American Psychoanalytic Association* 12 (October 1962).

The dramatist cannot be content merely to present phantasies (or fantasies either), he must arrange them in significant progression. It is Dr. Kligerman's thesis, I take it, that the three main phantasies constitute a dramatic beginning, middle, and end. The question is: of what? That they make up the beginning, middle, and the end of the six characters' own story is pretty clear. Does that make them the beginning, middle, and end of the whole work? Rather naturally giving psychology priority over dramatic art, our psychoanalytic interpreter seems to answer this in the affirmative, and backs up his answer with biographical rather than artistic evidence. "The Father, Son and Boy," says Dr. Kligerman, "all represent different levels of conflict within the author." This may well be a true statement on the *sources* of the matter presented. It does not follow that the three characters, once created, are best considered as three aspects of one character. All the characters a playwright "creates" come out of himself, just as his dreams do, and may similarly correspond to parts of himself. The important thing, artistically, is that they then become objectified, and demand to be seen not as aspects of their author but as his creations. If this is true, our protagonist in *Six Characters* has real others (not himself in other forms) to act upon and be acted upon by. This is a man and his son, not a man and himself, though, biologically and symbolically, a man and his son are overlapping categories.

And the end of the family story is not, as I think Dr. Kligerman assumes, the death of the two children, but the situation that ensues thereon. It is described thus in the first edition:

> Because, finally, the drama is all in this: when the mother re-enters my home, the family she had elsewhere, which was now being, as it were, superimposed on the first one, comes to an end, it's alien, it can't grow in this soil. The little girl dies, the little boy comes to a tragic end, the older girl flees. And so, after all the torment, there remain we three—myself, the mother, the son. And when the alien family is gone, we too find ourselves alien, the one to the other. We find ourselves utterly desolated.

The Father is given these words toward the end of Act One.* Later Pirandello must have concluded both that the passage comes at the wrong place and that it is too explicit. He put it off to the very end of the play and did the job without words: the final version states in a stage direction that father, mother, and son are left on stage at the end

---

*I should perhaps say "Section One," as the Italian editions have no act divisions. But many Americans know the play from a translation that names the sections Acts.

when the daughter rushes out of their home. They form a tableau with the mother's arms outstretched toward the obdurate son. Which I take to mean that the death of the two children is not the final phantasy. Rather, the dramatist insists on returning to the Oedipal image: the family story begins and ends with father, mother, and son. The daughter and two younger children came and went. Their father had gone forever just before we meet them. *The second family is killed off.* We see the effect upon the first family which lives on, bearing the brunt.

So far I have been talking exclusively of the six characters' story, which is complete (as complete as it is going to be) before the show starts: it is all time past. Does nothing happen on stage except a re-enactment of this past? Does nothing happen before our eyes and now, for the first time, in the present? Certainly it does. The six characters enter a theatre and ask the Director to make a play of them. He toys with the idea, finds himself, indeed, devoting the day to trying it out. A negative decision is reached, and that is the end. The first edition actually closes with the line, and it is a very good curtain line: *"E mi hanno fatto perdere una giornata!"*—"And they've made me lose a whole day."*

I am describing now, of course, the conceit or *trovata* which gave the play fame, and even notoriety, the idea of an encounter between a company of actors and the roles they might be asked to play. Can it be disposed of lightly? "The plot of the play within a play," Dr. Kligerman says, "contains the essential drama, for the rest is comic badinage . . . and a great deal of discussion. . . ." If valid, this would be a devastating criticism: no dramatic masterpiece would have so much dead wood in it. Conversely, if this is a great play, expressive in all its parts, then both the "badinage" and the "great deal of discussion" will be found to be necessary to its structure. Let us look further into the matter.

Drama is action. "An encounter between a company of actors and the roles they might play": this is a formula for action, but as it stands it is too general. Action has to be more specific than that. Who is doing what to whom? We have always to come to this question. Take the first bit of it first: *who is doing?* It needs hardly a moment's reflection on *Six Characters in Search of an Author* to produce an answer that comes from an overpowering impression. *The Father is doing.* If an Action is

---

*Pirandello's countryman Suetonius wrote about Titus: "Recalling that he had not granted a single favor all day, he [said]: 'I have lost a day.' "

here being propelled forward by a character, then that propeller is the Father. He is indeed so maniacally insistent that he might seem at times to be lifting the play up bodily. His insistency is a huge motif, and a huge portion of the play. *What* is he doing? He is demanding that his drama be staged. Why? He is persuaded that he will be thereby justified. A hostile interpretation of his character will be rejected, a friendly one endorsed. Does he really believe this? It is hard to say. He is so intent on stressing what should be, it is hard to know if he is confident that it will be. If he gets nowhere, will he settle for less? It looks very much as if the less that he will settle for is the act of pleading itself. He evidently gets a release from just talking, from unburdening himself. He is, among other things, an Ancient Mariner, buttonholing people and inflicting his story on them. And one knows what satisfaction all Ancient Mariners get from this kind of thing, because every one of us is something of an Ancient Mariner. For this mariner, certainly, saying his piece is a matter of life and death. I am reminded of a patient cited in R. D. Laing's book *The Divided Self* as saying that he talked as an act of self-preservation. That is to imply that his existence was threatened. And the sense of such a threat is felt in all the big talking in Pirandello—that of his Henry IV, that of his Ponza and Frola, and that of the Father. The topic, here, is schizophrenia, and Pirandello's plays have become easier to comprehend in the light of studies of schizoid problems written in the past several decades.

It is interesting that in two generations a great dramatist has led the psychologists in providing a classic image of modern man. Ibsen, just before Freud, presented Modern Man as Neurotic. Pirandello, anticipating the study of schizophrenia by a whole school of psychiatrists from Minkowski to Laing, showed how integral to modern life is "the schizophrenic experience." His Henry IV is the schizophrenic as tragic hero.

> . . . the experience and behavior that gets labelled schizophrenic is a special strategy that a person invents in order to live in an unlivable situation.*

In *Right You Are*, the Ponza/Frola narrative is an elaboration of such a special strategy, neither more nor less. Such strategies constitute the sanity of the insane, the rationality of the irrational. That is one paradox which Pirandello has in common with recent psychologists. Another is that the sane may not be any more rational. So one can regard

*R. D. Laing, *The Politics of Experience* (New York: Pantheon), 1967.

the insane as sane, and the sane as insane. The thought is no longer new, but new testimony to its truth is printed in each day's newspaper.

What is the Father doing? He is talking to live—that is, to avoid getting killed. He is fighting off the arrows of the Indian hordes of the soul. The world's *implosion*, Dr. Laing calls that kind of threat. The Father is also trying to keep from drowning, from inundation. Dr. Laing speaks of *engulfment*. Like a witch doctor, the Father hopes to hold the devils and hobgoblins at arm's length. In short, he is what our grandparents called a lunatic. He is "mad as a hatter." Critics and actors who have resisted this conclusion have never got very far with *Six Characters in Search of an Author*.

Yet the Father's manic behavior on stage is the least of it. In drama, as in life, character is found in concentrated form in men's decisions and actions which entail decisions. What have been this man's decisions? Since he is nothing if not a father and a husband, we must ask what he has done for his son and wife. When the former was a baby he sent him into the country to be nursed. It would be healthier. This is a rich man who prefers the ways of the poor. But when does he have his son brought back? We are not told, except that it was too late. The boy returned as an alien and an enemy. And the wife? He pushed her into the arms of his secretary. These, too, were good, simple people—also poor—who understood each other. The Father's actions have been such as to destroy his own family by driving them away. Obviously, he is what is usually called schizophrenic, and must isolate himself, even though isolation, in turn, becomes torture. If he can't stand company, equally he cannot stand himself. Desperate measures are taken against the outer world on behalf of the inner world, but to no avail. The inner world feels as insecure as ever, and the Father goes out in search of . . . well, in the first instance, company.

He becomes a client of Madama Pace's, the Pacifying Madam. What, in external terms, goes wrong at her place we know. What does it all signify? Again, it suffices to look closely at the specific data. His wife he considered motherly but asexual. Madama Pace is a mother who sells sex. She is motherhood degraded, and she is sex degraded. As Dr. Kligerman has noticed, she is the "giantess of the nursery," the castrating nanny, and, according to the first version, carries scissors. Perhaps it was defensiveness that made Pirandello omit the scissors from the revised text; surely they are a vivid touch. And the Stepdaughter, whatever else she is, is the Mother when young, the Mother with sex appeal, as in *Enrico IV*, where the Emperor embraces the daughter instead of the mother. What is the substance of the encoun-

ter at Madama Pace's? The evil mother offers our man a girl. The girl
says: My father just died. The man says: Take your dress off. The good
mother rushes in, crying: Stop, that's my daughter! A hideous little instrument of self-torture, this phantasy, though no more so than a
thousand others in the chronicles of schizophrenia.

In nothing is the complexity of Pirandello's dramaturgy more evident than in this creation, Madama Pace. She is not one of the six
characters. She is conjured up by the spirit of the theatre on the initiative of the Father. What does he mean by this initiative, and what does
his author mean? *Six Characters in Search of an Author* can be conceived
of as many concentric circles, in which case Madama Pace might well
be the innermost circle: play within play within play within
play . . . Now the most helpful insight into plays within plays—or
rather dreams within dreams—has been Freud's. He remarked that we
dream we are dreaming when we especially wish to disown a particular
phantasy as "only a dream." And the phantasies we particularly wish
to disown present what troubles us most in a rather blunt form. Madama Pace is not one of the actors, she is not one of the six, she is conjured up by one of the six, or by his "idea of a theatre." Most likely (as
psychoanalysts will suggest) she is what troubles Pirandello. Certainly
she is what troubles the Father: his mother as "giantess of the nursery,"
as castrator. Above all, as procuress—provider and degrader of sexual
pleasure. The Father is this play's Dr. Faustus, and she is his bad angel.

If she is a go-between, between whom does she go? Between the two
families that the six characters consist of. And the story of the six can
usefully be seen as a confrontation of these two groups, the legitimate
and the illegitimate, pursuing licit and illicit love. Each of the three
traumatic situations I have described brings the two groups into desperate conflict: father with his wife's illegitimate daughter, adulterous
mother with the legitimate son, illegitimate younger children with the
legitimate son. It is appropriate to this play that one finds oneself pro-
posing different ways of looking at it. Each way is likely to have its peculiar advantage. And the schema just provided has the advantage of
bringing out the special importance of the Son. He "dominates" two of
the bad situations, and is not outside the third one (since he reacts
strongly to the "incest"). When we speak of sibling murder, we can cite
the Son as the murderer of both younger children.

If the confrontation of the legitimate and the illegitimate families is
important to the structure of the play, what of the confrontation we
began to look into a few minutes ago, that of the family with the theatrical troupe? Of all the concentric circles, this is perhaps the outermost

one. Which in itself might tend to make a psychiatrist regard it as the least important, since the doctor's job is to look for hidden disease and penetrate disguises. Art, however, is not a disease, and in theatre art the disguise is in a clear sense the *ding an sich*. Nor—contrary to what many academic as well as clinical critics assume—does the artist harbor a general prejudice in favor of hidden meanings and against obvious ones. On the contrary, the weight to be given to the most external of the dramas in *Six Characters* must be decided without prejudice against externality. It is wholly a question of what weight, by his own artistic means, did Pirandello give to it.

Well, to begin with, he derived the title of the whole work from it, and considering how unerring his intuition was apt to be in such matters, this "small" item should not be overlooked. Granted that the substance of Action in the work is inner, neurotic, and even schizophrenic experience, what of the ever-present fact that the vehicle of Action is this conceit: characters in search of an author? It is a search with two aspects: the wish for a play to be *written* and the wish for it to be *enacted*. Let us take the second aspect first.

Enactment. If there is anything we are not in doubt about after we have seen this play it is that, for its author, all the world is a stage. *Totus mundus facit histrionem*, as the motto of the Globe Theatre read. But the idea receives a specific application here that is not so obvious. What happens when the actors try to enact the *scene* in Madama Pace's shop? They fail. But the point of the passage is lost when the actors are presented as inept. That kind of failure has too little content. A bad actor is a bad actor, period. What relationship does Pirandello define between the real thing and the re-enactment? Is it not that of a translation that cannot in the nature of things be a faithful one? The best analogy I can find is with the attempt to reconstruct a dream with the aid of notes jotted down upon waking. The notes are very definite, perhaps; but they are fragmentary. There are gaps, and above all the tone of feeling that characterized the whole world of the dream has gone. The Pirandellian re-enactment is incomplete and deeply unsatisfying in just this way.

But enactment is only an offshoot anyway, an offshoot of what is to be enacted: the author's work. IN CERCA D'AUTORE. And *who* is searching for him? Six characters? Not really. There is no evidence that the two children think themselves engaged in such a search. Like children generally, they are dragged along. The older boy definitely objects to the search, practices civil disobedience against it: that is what breaks up the experiment, and precipitates the end of the play.

The mother is distressed by the experiment, and gets dragged in against her will. That leaves just two characters who do search for an author—the Father and the Stepdaughter. And only these two had previously pleaded with the author who created them to make them part of a complete work of art:

> . . . trying to persuade him, trying to push him . . . I would appear before him sometimes, sometimes she would go to him, sometimes that poor mother . . . *(The Father)*

> . . . I too went there, sir, to tempt him, many times, in the melancholy of that study of his, at the twilight hour when he would sit stretched out in his armchair, unable to make up his mind to switch the light on, and letting the evening shadows invade the room, knowing that these shadows were alive with us . . . *(The Stepdaughter)*

Even the Stepdaughter has only a conditional interest in finding an author, the condition being that the Father insists on finding him. Then she will meet the challenge. The Father is the challenger: it is his project. And the play *Six Characters in Search of an Author* is his play—not in the sense that other characters are aspects of him but in the sense that he is consistently the prime mover. The story of the six starts from his actions—in marrying, in becoming a father, but even more in driving wife and son out. It starts again from his actions on the death of his rival: meeting the daughter at Madama Pace's, taking the family back into his house. The various family catastrophes stem from him. He is the base of that Oedipal triangle on which the family story rests. Last—and, to a dramatic critic, not least—he takes the initiative in the new and present Action. Our play begins with the arrival of the Father at the theatre, and from then on what we are witnessing is the encounter of the Father with the *Capocomico*. The latter is a Director, not an Author—yet another of the play's special twists—but the question before us is whether he will take on a writer's chores and write, as well as direct, the play into which the six characters would properly fit. As soon as he has decided not to, "our play is done," and Father's Day is over.

It is odd that anyone should speak of character conflicts in *Six Characters* without mentioning the one that stands in the foreground and works its way out of the primary Action. I suppose it could only happen because of that prejudice in favor of the secret and murky that I was speaking of. In itself the confrontation Father/Director is an archetypal affair: the confrontation of pathetic suffering humanity with the authorities. And these authorities are portrayed, in almost Shavi-an fashion, not as hostile and malicious but as open-natured, well-meaning, and far more reasonable than suffering humanity. It is true they are also smug, a little stupid, and very much out of contact—theirs is the life-style of bureaucrats and organization men.

Which would just be a picture of normal experience except that Pirandello pushes it, in his usual manner, far beyond the normalities; and Father and Director come to embody two sides of a schizophrenic situation. Through the Father we glimpse the inner world of modern man, through the Director, the outer. Both these worlds are shown as spiritually impoverished. The inner world of the Father contains nothing much besides his two or three phantasies and the pain he feels in failing to justify himself. The Director's outer world is reduced to rituals that preserve the appearances and maintain the occasion, habits, routines, clichés. *All that either the Father or the Director do is repeat themselves,* a factor which is close to the central metaphor of the play: life as theatre. Which aspect of theatre is exhibited in this play? Not performance. Only rehearsal—*répétition.* The stage is bare. The auditorium is empty. The theatre, too, is impoverished and deprived. The bourgeois drama, which had become thrilling through a kind of claustrophobic tension, here dissolves in agoraphobia, its opposite.

What is the Father seeking in the Director? An author who will put him in a play and justify him. In what sense "justify"? First of all, defend him from the Stepdaughter's charge of bestiality by citing the sexual needs of middle-aged men living apart from their wives, and so on. Is that all? Nothing in *Six Characters* is ever all. If the plot has an outermost circle, the theme hasn't. It reaches out toward infinity, a place where there is either emptiness or God. It should not be too surprising that a great play of dead or agonized fatherhood reverberates with the sense of God the Father, or rather of his absence—the "death of God." A search for an author can easily suggest a search for the Author of our being, and the main metaphor of the play has reminded some people of Calderón's *El gran teatro del mundo.* I only wonder they haven't commented on the opening words of that work: *"Sale el Autor . . . ."* "Enter the Author in a starry mantle with nine rays of light in groups of threes on his hat." This is, of course, God.

It is not necessary to assume that Pirandello had Calderón in mind, or that he thought directly of God at all. God is meaning, God is authority and authorship, God is fatherhood. A poignant sense of the absence of all these burns through every page of *Six Characters in Search of an Author.*

To me, the deepest—or perhaps I mean soundest—interpretation of the search for an author would stress neither God nor literary authorship but fatherhood, and I like to think I derive this choice, not from personal predilection, but from the text. The concisest way of stating what the Father demands of the Director in human terms—and Pirandello is always in search of the centrally human—is to say he is asking him to be his father. "Father me." "Rescue me from this maniacal female." "Tell me what is so, reassure me, help me find my place in the story, in the scheme of things, take from me this burden which I cannot bear but which you can." And the Director is very much the daddy of his troupe: that is established at his first entrance. But being the daddy of these lightweight Thespians is one thing, taking on suffering, schizoid humanity is another, particularly in the case of one who calls himself "Father" and should be able to fend for himself. In any event, the Director is another very inadequate Father. Something of a grotesque, he stands in the same relationship to fatherhood as Madama Pace does to motherhood. (Father, Director, Secretary-Lover: three fathers. Mother, Pace, Stepdaughter: three mothers. Another of this play's many symmetries.) But while she castrates, he is castrated: he has the character of the traditional impotent old clown. Our intellectual author transposes this impotence to the literary plane where the Director can prove impotent to make art from the Father's life, life from the Father's art.

In one respect the word "author" is exactly right in suggesting just what a "father" might be expected to provide. When the Father finds the right playwright he will not be content to be given some dialogue in which he can rapidly discomfit his stepdaughter. His ambition goes far beyond that. He is not even saying, "Write a melodrama, and make me the hero." He is saying, "A person is an entity with no clear meaning—an entity close to nonentity—unless there is an author to make him part of (a part in) a play."

A severed hand, Aristotle has it, is not a hand at all, because it could function as a hand only by belonging to arm and body. A character severed from a play is not even a character. A person severed from his family is not even a person. But what is he? And what can he do about it? We need to watch the words and actions of the Father to find the answer to such questions. Is the Father's quest as hopeless as the effort to graft a hand back onto an arm? Or is success in the quest within the power of an Author—in one sense or another of the word "author"? This is not a play that provides answers. At any rate, it is not a play that provides positive answers. But neither is it a play in

71

which the objects of yearning have been eliminated. Nostalgia pervades it. Nostalgia for what? For some kind of "togetherness." Is this just a regressive fantasy, the longing for the union of embryo and mother? *Child* and mother? There is something here of the modern isolated individual's longing for a social community, but again it is a longing directed backward toward some golden age, not forward toward a new society. By consequence, it is a fantasy not of freedom but of freely accepted bondage.

If only the Father could be part of a play, so he explains in the terms of Pirandello's literary conceit, he would have the permanence of Sancho Panza or Don Abbondio. Interpreting the play, we might translate this back into terms of life, thus: *to have a part in a play* means *to be a member of a family*, and the family is seen as an organism in which each cell lives in and by a happy interdependence. Before such a family could exist, the kind of life we find in Pirandello's play would need to be enormously enriched. It requires a texture far finer than phantasy and fear and guilt can provide. God is love; Father, too, would have to be love. That is the kind of Father this Father is in search of in a play which might just as well be called *A Father in Search of a Father*.

The crowning, and Pirandellian, irony comes when the Director's contribution to the proposed "drama," instead of enriching it, actually impoverishes it further. I am speaking of his work on the *scene* in Act Two. What he starts from is a piece of raw life, or rather a piece of raw erotic phantasy. Give this bit of life or phantasy to a Shakespeare, in the age of Shakespeare, and it becomes *Antony and Cleopatra* with noble enough roles in it for many. All our Director can do is convert it into what in America we would call Broadway drama, in which the already attenuated naturalism of the *scene* has to be further attenuated in the interests of middle-class entertainment.

Shakespeare proves in *Hamlet* that the schizophrenia of an Ophelia can be part of a grand design. Pirandello is interested in showing that in life she would encounter someone like the Director in *Six Characters* or the Doctor in *Enrico IV*. That is to say, she would be on her own. Which is what schizophrenia is. Art is sane. Life is schizoid; and offers only schizoid solutions, as in *Right You Are*. In *Enrico IV*, the schizoid solution is a starting point, then the "sane" people break it to pieces, as it is always the itch of "sane" people to do. One must reckon with this itch in the Director and Actors in *Six Characters*. Yet the play exhibits neither a solution nor a cataclysm—only a constantly re-enacted phantasy, a father journeying endlessly onward like the Flying Dutchman.

72

Now what the Dutchman was searching for was love. Is the Father's aim all that different?

This is the point at which that "great deal of discussion" which Dr. Kligerman complains of can perhaps be comprehended, for the bulk of it consists of long speeches made by the Father. If, as most critics have assumed, they are really there as exposition of a philosophy, then surely they will be an unwelcome intrusion. What is their content? I'd say that two main points are made, one directed at the Stepdaughter (particularly toward the end of Act One), one directed at the Director (particularly at the beginning of Act Three). The first point is that personality is not unitary but multiple. The second point is that illusion *is* reality. In the context it is not essential that these topics be regarded as interesting in themselves. They are dramatized. Which is to say, they become Action. Just as talking is something the Father has to do to live, so resorting to the particular "talking points" he makes is a matter of urgent necessity for him. If the theory of multiple personality did not exist he would have to invent it. It gets him off the hook on which the incident at Madama Pace's had hung him.

He is not necessarily right, however, even though his view coincides with the author's philosophy. From the point of view of drama, I would hold that he is wrong. For the art of drama, as Aristotle explained, takes for granted that actions do define a character. A man *is* what he does at Madama Pace's, and all his talk about really being otherwise is so much . . . well, talk. Whatever Pirandello may have believed, his dramas are drama, and present people as their actions. True, talking is an action—the Father's principal action most of the time—but it is precisely his compulsive talking that inclines us not to accept the endless self-pity and self-justification at face value. The Father *feels* that he is many and not one. But that, as we blithely say, is "*his* problem." He is a very irresponsible man, if sane; and, if not responsible for his actions, then insane. On either assumption, he needs just the philosophy Pirandello gives him. Nothing diffuses responsibility more conveniently than the theory that one is a succession of different people. And if one is insane, one is surely entitled to complain a good deal of that radical disjunction which is one's fate. One may even project it on everyone else.

Freud compares paranoid fantasies to metaphysical systems. It is a comparison that makes some sense in reverse. The Pirandellian metaphysics provides apt fantasies for his mentally disturbed characters.

I gave as the Father's second philosophic idea that illusion is reality. Which is also "what everybody knows about Luigi Pirandello." To say that illusion is reality is, on the face of it, nonsense but can be construed as sense by taking it paradoxically. It is as a paradox that the notion has its primary use to Pirandello. For paradoxes, when expanded, become comedies. The expansion happens, in Pirandello, by doubling and redoubling. Take, in our play, the opposites *life* and *art*. The actors are from *life*. The characters are from *art*. However, nothing begins to "pop" as comedy, as drama, until the author reverses the proposition. The characters are more *real*, are therefore portrayed more as what we regard as people from *life*: they have instincts, impulses, private lives. The actors are less real, and are therefore portrayed as artifacts, as "types," as creatures out of a play. In short, the actors are from art. The characters from life. What one might call the intellectual comedy of *Six Characters in Search of an Author* is built upon this reversibility of the key terms. And what is the truth? Which is "really" life, and which is "really" art? There Pirandello-Laudisi lies in wait for us—laughing. Everything in his little system (or *game*, if we must be up-to-date) works both ways. Nothing is "really" so, because everything is "really" so.

Now a person making use of this system—a person playing this game—can have everything both ways. Which is a very nice way to have everything: it is what we all want, though in proportion as we cease to be childish or sick we learn to do without a good deal of what we all want. The Father, however, *is* childish and sick. The Pirandellian game is after his own heart. In Act Two, he is essentially telling the actors to subordinate their *art* to *life*. All that is wrong with their performance is that it isn't naturalistic, it isn't exactly what happened in Madama Pace's shop. But in his theoretical vein, he usually exalts art *above* life. Similarly, he can use the word "illusion" in a pejorative sense, as when he tells the Director that the actors' lives are more an illusion than the characters' lives, while in the same breath speaking of illusion with respect and a kind of nostalgic awe. All of this is word play, word *game*, inconclusive, and in principle endless—and therefore very depressing. Pirandello can call Laudisi-ism "deviltry" and ask for a comedic tone, but it is black comedy at best: its underside is despair. Pursue any statement the Father may offer as consolation and you will find it lets you down with a bump. For example: art as a solution to the bafflements of impermanence. As a statue you can live forever. The only thing is: you're dead. Petrifaction is no answer, but only corresponds to yet another schizoid wish. And anyone who knows this particular Father will quickly sense that his wish to be a work of art is his wish to escape from flesh and blood—that is, from life. As with other schizophrenics, the great fear of being killed does not prevent him from yearning for death. Indeed it is at this stage of the argument that we realize that the Father's two main points have, for him, the same point: he wants to get out of his own skin. He is "one." But he cites as an alibi that nobody is one, we are each of us a hundred thousand. He is real. But he cites as an alibi that nobody is real. He is trying to non-exist. His personality can, as it were, be diffused horizontally, losing itself in moments or states of mind, alleged other personalities. Or it can be diffused vertically in vapors of idea. But total nonexistence is too terrifying to flatly accept. One has to try and coax it into acceptability. By paradox. By dialectic. All of which is evasion, though, for a schizophrenic, a necessary evasion.

"If the self is not true to itself, it is in despair," says Kierkegaard. Pirandello depicts a despair so deep that his schizophrenics cannot afford to admit they have selves to be untrue to. The theory of multiple personality is a byproduct of the despair, and, for the Father, a necessary fiction.

The very notion that illusion is reality stems from defeatism. Philosophically, it represents the breakdown of the Hegelian tradition in which there was always a reality to offset appearances. Once the reality starts to be eroded, there will eventually be nothing left but the appearances; and at this point in time philosophers start to advocate *accepting facts at face value*—face value is the only value they have or the world has. Hence, for example, a contemporary of Pirandello's who later became the house philosopher of Mussolini, Giovanni Gentile, wrote in 1916: "The truth is what is in the making."*

In this respect, there are only two interpretations of *Six Characters in Search of an Author*. According to one, the play itself endorses Gentile, endorses the Father's philosophic utterances. According to the other, which I subscribe to, the play is larger than the Father, "places" him in a larger setting, makes his pathos unsympathetic. I am not going to argue that the play embodies a positive faith. A critic who did this had to rely upon a single sentence that is present only in the first edition.** I am arguing that it is not a philosophical play at all because the philosophy is harnessed to a nonphilosophical chariot. The content is psychopathological from beginning to end.

Perhaps I've said overmuch about psychological motifs. This is an exuberant, excessive, Sicilian work, and from perhaps overmuch suggestiveness may easily come overmuch critical suggestion. Let my last comments be about the form of the work. The first thing a traditional

*The Theory of Mind as Pure Act (New York: Macmillan, 1922).
**La giara e altre novelle, a cura di Giuseppe Lanza (Milan, 1965), p. 15.

critic—if such a person still exists—would notice about this search for an author is that it respects the unities of time, place, and action. In other words, it conspicuously possesses that compact and classic dramatic structure which the "play in the making" (with its story of the six) conspicuously lacks. The space of time covered is literally the time spent in the theatre plus enough extra hours or minutes to permit the Director to call the session a "whole day"—if we must take *him* literally. Place is given in an equally literal way. And there is something Pirandellian in the fact that such literalness could be a brainstorm. What earned the Maestro the highest compliments for originality was that in his work the boards of the theatre represent—the boards of the theatre. That is to say, they do not represent, they are. They are appearances which are the reality: the quintessential Pirandellian principle.

The final point of this handling of place is a dialectical one. The boards of the theatre are to be so definite, so "real" because the "real" streets of the town and country, the gardens, the houses and rooms are to be so shadowy, so "unreal." The interaction of these two elements gives Pirandello a goodly part of his play—and a good deal that is peculiar to his play.

Time also is handled dialectically. Over against this flatly undistorted present on the stage is the story of the six, all of which is already past. The six are trying to pull all this baggage of theirs, as the patient does on the doctor's couch, from the dim, anesthetic past into the garish, stinging present. The past of the six and the present of the acting troupe are so clearly demarcated that some people see only the one, some only the other, whereas, to realize what Pirandello is up to, we not only have to see both but the constant reaction of one upon the other. There is a further complication. The past and present of the six are *not* clearly demarcated, but, on the contrary, are deliberately mingled, as in dreams. Hence, for example, though the Stepdaughter has already left her parents, here she is back with them, and the younger children, who have died, are alive again. They will die again, and the play will end with the Stepdaughter leaving her parents. . . . But I am afraid that in turning from content to form, I have *been turned back*, by the work itself, from form to content.

One last notation. By an error which was to create a possibly permanent misunderstanding, *Six Characters in Search of an Author* in its first edition was subtitled: "a play in the making."* But the play in the

*The Italian original reads: *"una commedia da fare."* In the translation most widely read in America, this has been rendered: "a comedy in the making." But in Italian, as in French, a *"commedia" (comédie)* is not necessarily comic, and the word should often

making is the projected play about the six characters that never gets made. The play that gets made is the play about the encounter of the six characters (seven, finally) with the Director and his acting troupe. This of course includes as much of the unwritten play as is needed. Finally, then, *Six Characters* becomes a play fully made. Bernard Shaw said he had never come across so original a play.*[It is a supreme contribution that says something profound about the theatre and about life seen as theatre and seen by means of the theatre. The originality should not blind us to the beauty of the form or to that existential anguish which is the content.]

---

be translated as a "play." (That the story of the six should turn out comic is out of the question.) Second, if the phrase "in the making" suggests, as I think it does, that there are the makings of a play in this material (which is the opposite of what Pirandello is saying), then it is a mistranslation of *"da fare,* which means, literally, "to make," and, less literally, "to be made," "yet to be made," "not yet made." Incidentally, "in the making" cited above Giovanni Gentile does not translate "da fare." Gentile's original reads: *"Vero è quel che si fa,"* which would be rendered literally: "True is that which is done."

*When Pirandello's preface to *Six Characters* was published in French translation (*Revue de Paris,* July 15, 1925), Pirandello added this paragraph (here literally translated) to the text:

If modesty forbids me to accept G. B. Shaw's assertion that Six Characters is the most original and most powerful work of all the theatres ancient and modern in all nations, I can't help being aware that their appearance in the history of the Italian theatre marks a date that people won't be able to forget.

When at a later date this passage was brought to Shaw's attention, he commented: "I have no recollection of the extravagant dictum you quote: but I rank P. as first rate among playwrights and have never come across a play so *original* as Six Chracters [sic]" (*The Shavian,* February 1964).

THE LIFE AND WORKS OF
LUIGI PIRANDELLO

1

Luigi Pirandello was born on June 28, 1867, near Agrigento in southern Sicily. As he himself put it, "I am the son of Chaos, and not allegorically but literally, because I was born in a country spot, called, by the people around, *Cavasu*, a dialectal corruption of the authentic, ancient Greek word, *chaos*." Pirandello's father was a sulphur-mine owner who had fought for Garibaldi in 1860 and 1862 and who, in 1863, had married the sister of one of his comrades in arms. Until he was nineteen, it looked as if Pirandello might spend his whole lifetime within the circle of family interests: he was to enter his father's line of business and he became engaged to his cousin Lina. But in 1886, when he returned from school in Palermo to his native Agrigento, he went back again to Palermo almost at once, and enrolled in literature courses at the university. Although his engagement lasted another three years, he was soon writing Lina sentiments which, far from expressing confidence in their relationship, voiced agonized doubts as to the possibility of any relationship at all. These doubts later came to be considered characteristically Pirandellian and some commentators lightheartedly considered them a vintage product of the 1920s:

> Meditation is the black abyss, populated by dark phantoms, watched over by desperate dejection. No ray of light ever pierces it: the desire for one only sinks you ever deeper in the dense shadows. . . . It is an insatiable thirst, an obstinate fury: but there's nothing to drink but the

blackness, and the silent immensity freezes you. We are like the poor spiders which, in order to live, need to weave their subtle web in some corner, we are like the poor snails which, in order to live, need to carry their frail shells on their backs, or like the poor mollusks which crave their conches at the bottom of the sea. We are spiders, snails, mollusks of a nobler race, to be sure, we wouldn't want a web, a shell, a conch, to be sure, but we would want a little world, oh yes, both to live in it and to live by it. An ideal, a feeling, a habit, an occupation—that's the little world, that's the shell of this giant snail or man as we call it. . . . I write and study to forget myself—to distract myself from despair.*

In 1887, Pirandello left the University of Palermo for the University of Rome, and in 1889, he went on to the University of Bonn in Germany, where he got his doctorate two years later with a dissertation on the dialect of his native Agrigento. In 1889 he also began publishing. Though his earliest literary career was that of a minor poet, by 1893 he was writing a novel, *The Outcast*. In 1894, unable to fulfill his engagement to his cousin Lina, he married the daughter of one of his father's associates, Maria Antonietta Portulano. The couple had three children: Stefano, born in 1895, Lietta, born in 1897, and Fausto, born in 1899; Fausto was to become one of the notable Italian painters of the twentieth century. In 1897, Pirandello began to work at a girls' school in Rome, l'Istituto Superiore di Magistero, which post he was not to leave until 1922.

He would undoubtedly have left much earlier but for an economic disaster that hit him and his wife in 1903. In that year a landslide destroyed the mine in which both his father's fortune and his wife's dowry were tied up. The marriage had been an "economic" one from the beginning, and now it was shattered by an economic disaster. Maria Antonietta was stricken with paralysis of the legs when she got the news, and, although her legs recovered after six months, she became a victim of paranoid jealousy, and was insane for the rest of her life, though her husband delayed committing her to an institution until 1919 (where she lived until 1959). What was to be Pirandello's only really famous novel was the fruit of this family crisis, *The Late Mattia Pascal* (1904).

There were other novels: *The Merry Go Round*, written in 1895, was published in 1902; *The Old and the Young* came out serially, 1906-8; *Her Husband*, the only Pirandello novel that still has not been published in English, was out by 1911; *Shoot* followed in 1915; *One, None, and a Hundred Thousand* was published in 1926. But until well after

*Letter to Lina, October 31, 1886. Published in 1961 in *Terzo programma*, n. 3.

World War I, Pirandello's reputation rested principally upon the many short stories he had been publishing since the early 1890s: *Loves Without Love* (1894); *Jests of Death and Life* and *When I Was Crazy* (1902); *Two-faced Erma* (1906); *Naked Life* (1911); *Trios* (1912); *The Two Masks* (1914); *The Trap* and *Grass in Our Garden* (1915); *Tomorrow Is Monday* (1917); *A Horse in the Moon* (1918); *Berecche and the War* and *The Carnival of the Dead* (1919). His playwriting also began in the 1890s. A one-act, *The Epilogue*, later called *The Vise*, was printed in 1898. In the following year he wrote a full-length play, *If Not Thus*, which was not staged until 1915. Indeed, it was not until the second decade of this century that Pirandello got over the modern writer's feeling of superiority to all things theatrical, a feeling he recaptured and exploited even later in *Six Characters in Search of an Author*.

His career as a practicing playwright really began in 1910, under some degree of suasion from the actor-manager Nino Martoglio, but it was not until the later war years that plays, one after the other, began to flow from Pirandello's pen: *Think of That, Giacomino!* (1916); *Right You Are, Cap and Bells,* and *The Pleasure of Honesty* (1917); *But It's Not Serious* and *The Game of Role Playing* (1918); *Man, Beast, and Virtue* (1919); *All for the Best, Like the First Time Only Better,* and *Mrs. Morley One and Two* (1920). "It was war that revealed the theatre to me," the playwright reported later, "mine is a theatre of war: the passions were unchained, and I made my living creatures suffer those passions on stage."

Pirandello was still a struggling playwright, however, when *Six Characters in Search of an Author* opened at the Teatro Valle in Rome on May 10, 1921. Of his previous plays only one—*Like the First Time Only Better,* which opened in Milan on March 24, 1920—had found full favor with its audience. *Six Characters*, at its opening in Rome, was a *succès de scandale,* and the author had to slip out of the theatre to wild cries of "madhouse." But the Milan opening that fall—September 27 at the Teatro Manzoni—was a shot heard round the world. Though banned in London by the Lord Chamberlain, through the good offices of Bernard Shaw and others, *Six Characters* reached a public there in February 1922, under the auspices of a technically private club. By November it was playing at the Fulton Theatre in New York and in 1923 it played Paris, Cracow, Prague, Amsterdam, Warsaw, Barcelona, and Athens; in 1924 it played Vienna, Berlin, Zagreb, and Tokyo.

Financially, Pirandello was at last able to abandon his uncongenial teaching post. For the last fourteen years of his life he pursued the career of an international theatre man. His second most important play, *Enrico IV (The Emperor)* followed right on the heels of *Six Characters.*

81

Enrico IV also enjoyed a broad international success. Pirandello traveled with his plays to a number of the principal countries where they were performed—France, the United States, Argentina, Brazil, Germany—and, in Italy in 1925, became artistic director of a new Teatro d'Arte di Roma, for which he entertained very high hopes.

But only the years 1921–25, if those, were a simple success story for Pirandello. Italy has a perennial and chronic problem with all attempts to found stable theatres, and even the small degree of stability achieved by the Mussolini regime (1922–43) was not extended to Pirandello's effort: as usual the *Duce* offered more flowery language than *lire.* What is a profounder pity is that Pirandello did not prove able to sustain the high standard of *Six Characters* and *Enrico IV* in his subsequent plays. Over the next decade a great many new plays were produced: *To Clothe the Naked* (1922); *The Life I Gave You* (1923); *Each in His Own Way* (1924); *Diana and Tuda* and *The Wives' Friend* (1927); *The New Colony* (1928); *About Either One or No One* and *Lazarus* (1929); *As You Desire Me* and *Tonight We Improvise* (1930); *To Find Oneself* (1932); *When One Is Somebody* (1933); *No One Knows How* (1935); *Giants of the Mountain* (unfinished, but posthumously produced in 1937). These plays are not without interest for students of Pirandello, but they have not unduly interested anyone else. *As You Desire Me,* scenario and adaptation by Gene Markey, did become a Greta Garbo film in 1932, but it was not a very good film, and no one has attempted another treatment since. There is Pirandello's own authority for regarding *Each in His Own Way* and *Tonight We Improvise* as making up a trilogy with *Six Characters* as part one, but the continuity is only thematic, and the second and third parts seem less an artistic outgrowth of the first than a discursive, at times garrulous, elaboration of it. For it is not just that Pirandello's later plays are less popular; most of them are far less intense, and fatally attempt to make up in bigness of intellectual intention what they lack in realized emotion.

There are biographical reasons for this artistic decline, and they have been worked out in some detail by Gaspare Giudice.* Pirandello's great creative period of the early 1920s fell between the commitment of his wife Maria Antonietta to a sanatorium in 1919, and the marriage, and consequent departure from Italy, of his daughter Lietta in 1921–22. It was preceded by the death of Pirandello's mother in 1915, the wartime imprisonment of his son Stefano by the Austrians, and his own father's coming to live with him just after the war. The departure of Maria Antonietta also meant the return home of Lietta,

*See below, pp. 91–95.

who had been driven out by the virulence of her mother's paranoia. Now while it is not to be expected that these facts, as baldly rehearsed here, can prove very much, it may be useful to report that Signor Giudice is able to prove a good deal by a more extended exposition of them. He shows that Pirandello was an unusually personal, confessional, autobiographical writer from beginning to end and that the power of his writing is a matter of exactly which moment in his private life it springs from. Events of the second decade of this century led to a brief period of maximum creativity at the beginning of the third decade. No such period was to occur again.

There are two other topics in Pirandello's later life that can hardly be overlooked: fascism and Marta Abba. Until Giudice's book came out, the story of Pirandello's membership in the Fascist party during the last dozen years of his life had never been fully told. There was understandable embarrassment among his family and friends, and even the present-day Italian editions of his writings have some remarkable political lacunae. Hardly to be overlooked is the fact that Pirandello is presumably the only winner of the Nobel Prize to destroy his gold medal. As his bibliographer, Manlio Lo Vecchio Musti, reported this event: "During the Ethiopian campaign, he gave to the country all the gold he had, including the medal of the Nobel Prize, a gesture that aroused in Sweden the indignation of the hypocrites and the imbeciles."

Pirandello's relationship with the Fascist party had its ups and downs. He is said to have torn up his membership card once in a fit of rage, and even to have vowed that he would never return to Italy. But he and Mussolini had exchanged compliments at the time he joined the party—a time when Italians of humane views were shocked by the murder of the anti-Fascist leader Giacomo Matteotti—and Pirandello's fascism grew more outrageous with the years. It reached a climax with a speech he delivered to the Italian Academy in rapturous praise of the Abyssinian invasion in general, and Mussolini in particular.*

Although marital infidelity was always the charge leveled at Pirandello by his sick wife, and he was exposed to what she regarded as constant temptation at the girls' school where he taught, it is clear that his

---

*Printed in *Quadrivio*, November 3, 1935; omitted from the collected works in Italian; first printed in English in the *Drama Review*, Summer 1969. One reason that Pirandello's political pronouncements are missing from bibliographies is that many of them were made in interviews, including such interviews in English as are found in *Living Age*, October 1, 1926, August 15, 1927, November 1930, January 1931, and *Pictorial Review*, October 1933.

private life was unusually solitary. There seem to have been only two girls in the period before his marriage—his cousin Lina and a German girl he fell in love with in Bonn, Jenny Schulz-Lander; no women at all in the period of his marriage up to Maria Antonietta's being committed; and, after that, just one—Marta Abba. In 1925, Abba was a young, unknown actress whom Pirandello brought from Milan to his new Teatro d'Arte. She was soon playing leads in his plays, old and new. The leads in some of the new plays—*Diana and Tuda, The Wives' Friend, As You Desire Me,* above all *To Find Oneself*—if not based on Abba's own personality, were at least shaped to fit it. Pirandello loved her, and left her the rights to nine of his last plays in his will. Yet she does not seem to have ever become his mistress. Reports of the singular chastity of the relationship reached Mussolini himself, and the only definitely anti-Fascist remark Pirandello was ever quoted as making was a comment on the *Duce's* asking why he didn't sleep with Abba. "He is vulgar," said the Maestro. Perhaps Pirandello's letters to Abba, when they are published, will clarify the relationship. For the present the critic can only associate this romance with the romantic but overly abstract quality of most of the last plays, noting that when passionate feeling entered Pirandello's work its source seems always to have been his immediate family—his wife, his parents, his children. If Marta Abba was his Beatrice, this was a modern Dante swayed less by the ideal vision than by hates and fears, compulsions and anxieties and, if sometimes also by love, then by filial or paternal affection.

Outwardly, his life was quiet. In his last years he lived a good deal in hotel rooms all over the Western world, but the following brief account describes a larger span of his life:

> I very rarely go to the theatre. By then, every evening, I am in bed. I get up in good time every morning and usually work till twelve. After lunch, usually, I get to my writing table at 2:30 and remain there till 5:30, but after the morning hours I don't do any more writing, unless it is urgently necessary; rather, I read or study. In the evening, after supper, I enjoy conversation with my small family, read the headlines and article titles in some paper or other; then to bed. As you see, there is nothing worthy of special mention about my life: it is all inside, in the work, and in my thoughts which . . . are not cheerful.

"*O si scrive o si vive,*" he liked to say. "Either you write or you live," and he was not in doubt as to his own choice.

He died in his house, 15 via Antonio Bosio, Rome, on December 10, 1936. Born in "Chaos," he died in what, for a recent Nobel Prizewinner, was obscurity, for the papers at the time were full of the news of the abdication of King Edward VIII of England, and the death of the great Italian was lost in the back pages. He had fallen sick while watching the filming of *The Late Mattia Pascal*. This novel had given voice to the crisis that had ended his life as a relatively happy family man. It describes an effort to become someone else: Mattia Pascal becomes Adriano Meis. Is it possible that as Meis killed Pascal, Pascal now killed Pirandello? The thought may be extravagant, but it is not un-Pirandellian.

2

Although, as has been suggested above, *Six Characters in Search of an Author* was a precipitate from Pirandello's family situation at the time it was written, the idea had been in the author's mind and heart for some time. Nardelli, his interviewer-biographer, says it was written in three weeks. But that it was at least ten years forming will be plain to any reader of the short story "Tragedy of a Character" (1911) and the two stories "Conversations with Characters" (1915). Among posthumous materials that have come out in the collected works (Volume 6, 1960) is the letter to his son Stefano cited on p. 60 above. The same volume contains a fragment from this projected, but never completed, novel, which demonstrates that Madama Pace's establishment was an integral part of the scheme from an early date; also that the setting, a detail never given in the play, is (or at least was) Rome.

The ideas of the play can be found, for that matter, in many earlier Pirandello works. Martin Esslin, in the *New York Times* of June 25, 1967, summed it up this way: "For Pirandello, more than any other playwright, has been responsible for a revolution in man's attitude to the world, in its way as significant as the revolution caused by Einstein's discovery of the concept of relativity. Pirandello has transformed the whole concept of *reality* in human relations." This is to put the matter too philosophically, as if Pirandello were a William James or an A. N. Whitehead, yet the word "attitude" suggests what is nearer the truth: that it is a matter of how we *confront* certain things, how we *feel* about them, what our *sense* of them is.

There is an indispensable clue within the text of *Six Characters* itself. A play is being rehearsed when the six characters arrive. It is not *Charley's Aunt*,* as in one American production, or some bit of fashionable

---

*It is legitimate that translators replace references unknown to their audience with familiar ones. But what the references mean to that audience should be what the original references meant to the original audience. When Pirandello invokes the sacred

chaff, as is implied in at least one printed summary. It is a play by Luigi Pirandello with a title that says everything: *The Game of Role Playing*, which seems all too near the bone in the 1970s. A recent essay by Robert Jay Lifton characterizes the younger generation in America today with the term "protean personality," while all during the 1960s individual behavior has more and more been judged as (to use the title of a best-seller in the field) *Games People Play.* The director in *Six Characters* leads off with a summary of *The Game of Role Playing*: "You beat eggs. And you think you have nothing more on your hands than the beating of eggs? Guess again. You symbolize the shell of those eggs . . . the empty form of reason without the content of instinct, which is blind. You are reason and your wife is instinct in the game of role playing. You play the part assigned you, and you're your own puppet—of your own free will." Now this is sound enough abstract summary of the sort that critics visit upon Pirandello, and which he was not always above visiting upon himself. But here it is ridiculed, satirized, distanced. We are confronted with an attitude to it and the attitude is as important as its own object.

The action of *Six Characters* might be characterized as "what came of interrupting the rehearsal of *The Game of Role Playing*." This action explores the aforementioned "attitude" in depth, that is, in drama or in conflicting passions. *Six Characters* is not a disquisition on role playing. It *is* role playing, concretely presented; and through the intensity of the author's passion, the virtuosity of his talent, and the synthesizing power of his genius, it amounts to a unified vision of life as role playing, and as such is an archetype of the twentieth-century imagination.

3

According to some accounts, the idea for *Enrico IV* came to Pirandello when he was thumbing through an illustrated magazine and happened upon a picture of a cavalcade. One account specifies that it was the Roman Hunt Club riding to Villa Doria in medieval costume, but Arthur Livingston, a translator of Pirandello, in his *Essays on Modern Italian Literature* has the Maestro giving a different version. "Henry IV has its origin in an episode of Italy's movie world during the manufacture [*sic*] of a now famous play. An Italian actor, called upon to as-

---

memory of Manzoni with a reference, in *Six Characters*, to the priest Don Abbondio, it is ludicrous to refer, instead, to the Three Musketeers, as is done in one published and performed translation.

sume the role of Dante, threw himself so wholly into his work that he broke down under strain. Thereafter, as Pirandello says, he was unable to 'de-Dantify' himself, and is to this day living a placid life in an Italian asylum as the immortal poet of Beatrice."

Another translator of Pirandello's, Benjamin Crémieux, tells what books the Maestro consulted about the German Emperor Henry IV.* But more significant than Pirandello's reading on the theme is his choice of it. He had been a student at the University of Bonn, and undoubtedly German culture exercised a powerful influence on him, perhaps even a fascination. The philosophy which people call "Pirandellian" could be regarded as his own little digest of the German contribution to metaphysics from Kant on. If we have heard, in our time, of a Rome-Berlin Axis, we might speak, as students of Pirandello, of a Palermo-Bonn axis, for Pirandello spent much spiritual energy endeavoring to fuse within himself the Sicilian and popular elements with the European and intellectual elements. He naturally makes his Henry a spokesman for German idealism, or "Pirandellianism."

Pirandello is wise enough to put into the play itself any historical details he wishes his audiences to be aware of, but he does assume the spectator's prior knowledge of "Canossa." "We shall not go to Canossa," Bismarck had said in Pirandello's lifetime. For any educated European, Canossa is a permanent symbol of Papal supremacy and its corollary, the subjection of the temporal to the ecclesiastical power. In the year 1077, eleven years after William the Conqueror set foot in England, the Holy Roman Emperor knelt two days in the snow at Canossa, doing obeisance to the Pope and begging his Holiness for an audience. His wife, Empress Bertha, knelt with him, and Bertha's mother Adelaide went with the Abbot of Cluny, another friendly witness, to plead with the Pope and his ally the Countess Matilda of Tuscany.

Such is the scene which has remained indelibly imprinted upon the memory of Europe. Or perhaps one should say upon the fantasy of Europe, for the incident did not actually signify—as it is often taken to—that in the Middle Ages emperors always took their orders from the Popes. There is evidence that this very emperor, Henry IV, knelt there not in sincere submission, but because it was the smart thing to do. In 1076, at Tribur, the German princes had proposed the deposition of Henry. In kneeling at Canossa, the latter was heading off the prospect of having to face his accusers. Pirandello draws on very little of this material, but does remind us that the pseudohumble Henry remained the Pope's fierce enemy and, in the year 1080, at Brixen, would declare Pope Gregory VII deposed. Pirandello was no doubt interested also in the insecurity of Henry's position—and the insecurity of a world in which not only the Pope but also the Emperor lived in daily danger of deposition.

If the Canossa symbol is clear, and the reference to Brixen at least understandable, all the history the reader need bother his head with concerns the situation of Henry in his childhood. Even at Canossa he is only twenty-six years old. He had succeeded to the throne as a child, and his mother, Agnes, had to be regent. But she had come under suspicion of adultery with Henry, Bishop of Augsburg. Pirandello adds a touch of his own in making one of the Pope's henchmen, Peter Damiani, actually point an accusing finger at the pair. Agnes is removed as regent, and Henry IV himself rules—under the tutelage of others, and especially of Hanno, Bishop of Cologne. Later, Adalbert, Bishop of Bremen, becomes Henry's chief adviser, and Pirandello brings up the curtain at the point where Adalbert, as Henry supposedly believes, has been driven away by rival bishops.

Pirandello does not work out any point-for-point analogy between the eleventh-century story and his twentieth-century one (the reader to whom a historical reference here or there means nothing need not feel he is missing clues). When Pirandello wishes his audience to know that Matilda of Tuscany corresponds to Matilda Spina he says so. He also lets it be known that while the historical Matilda of Tuscany was simply the enemy of the Emperor, "our" Henry harbors a secret love for her. . . and so on.

The play is, after all, about the twentieth century. It is, in particular, a study in insanity, and while we need not take Pirandello too literally as a pathologist, he stays, in essentials, close to well-known symptoms. Here are two sentences about insane delusions from Bernard Hart's standard introduction to the subject, *The Psychology of Insanity:* "Delusions may be of all kinds, but there are two types which call for special mention on account of their great frequency, *grandiose* and *persecutory.* . . . The two types are frequently combined; for example, a patient may maintain that he is the king but that an organized conspiracy exists to deprive him of his birthright."

Pirandello himself may not have been committed to the "absolute relativism" which is preached by his protagonists. His plays imply objective standards, as perhaps plays have to. They imply a clear distinction between delusion and non-delusion. Without such a distinction, it would be meaningless to say that Henry ceased being mad after twelve years. Similarly, in the play which professes in its Italian title that a thing "*is* so if it seems so" to anyone, it is definitely implied that "seeming" may be an unreliable guide to truth, since the person to whom something seems thus and so may be crazy.

No major playwright has ever dealt chiefly in opinions per se. The playwright deals in experience—and therefore in opinions only insofar as they are not merely spoken or held, but experienced. The doubts about reality and identity with which *Six Characters* bristles are less a philosophical than a psychological matter, and Dr. Charles Kligerman in his essay "A Psychoanalytic Study of Pirandello's *Six Characters in Search of an Author*"* has shown that even a narrowly clinical approach to that play can be illuminating. Some of the very same clinical "material" is present in *Enrico IV*, notably the fantasy of a father embracing his daughter, and indeed the whole play can reasonably be taken as a realistically intended study of both neurotic and psychotic phenomena. If anyone seriously doubts this, let him reread the expository part of Act One, particularly what Belcredi and Matilda say about themselves and about Henry. The language may not be that of psychiatry in the second half of the twentieth century; but the content is close to, say, R. D. Laing's *The Divided Self*,** Alexander Lowen's *Betrayal of the Body*, Ernest Becker's *The Denial of Death*, and David Holbrook's *Gustav Mahler and the Courage to Be*.

It even makes sense to set aside the talk of "relativity" and conclude at the end that Henry *is* insane, that the unlucky experiment, though it went wrong, has produced the result that was feared and driven him back into insanity; the experiment, that is, plus the unfortunate turn taken by the conversation after it. What, after all, is going on? It is not possible to take the murder of Belcredi as one is invited to take the murder of Claudius in *Hamlet*, namely, as a just retribution willed by God. It is naked revenge at best, and committed in a peculiarly ignoble, unimperial way: would the medieval Emperor have run an unarmed man through—and, at that, through the belly? (It sounds more like Eilert Løvborg's suicide in *Hedda Gabler*.) One should not see the ending of this play as "romantic" and of vague import, or as a rather forced illustration of a metaphysical thesis, but just as what it brutally seems—either immoral or insane, most probably the latter. In either case, Pirandello's *Hamlet*—and the play might be considered such—is a modern *Hamlet*, an anti-*Hamlet*, a savage and serious parody. It is not tragedy but tragi-comedy, and it belongs to the modern and extreme form of this genre: tragic farce.

*See p. 62ff. above.
**See pp. 65-66 above.

In its substance, *Enrico IV* is not *merely* psychological; not, at any rate, in the limited terms of the psychoanalytic journals. To understand Pirandello, one would need a psychology with a psyche—a psychology which finds in the traditional terms "spirit" and "soul" a good deal more than can be reduced to the sexual mishaps of infancy or later. Pirandello writes of a sickness of the human creature that can scarcely be ascribed solely to the misadventures of the bedroom or the nursery. To diagnose this sickness one would need the instruments of disciplines other than the clinical; and even within the field of psychology, men of religious interests and deep intuition might offer more help in interpreting Pirandello than those who rely solely on current therapeutic science. St. Augustine, for instance, said: "Every disordered spirit is a punishment to itself," which might stand as an adequate motto for *Enrico IV.* Less summary, but even more suggestive by way of analogy and illustration, is this passage from William James: "One evening there fell upon me without warning a terrible fear of my own existence. There arose in my mind the image of an epileptic patient whom I had seen in the asylum, a blackhaired youth with greenish skin, looking absolutely nonhuman. That shape am I, I felt, potentially."

GASPARE GIUDICE'S BIOGRAPHY

Biographically speaking, there are three kinds of great writers: those like Strindberg who tell all,* those like Shakespeare who tell nothing, and third the vast majority who, telling less than all but more than nothing, can have their "story" figured out by scholars, if the latter have the patience to do the figuring and the skill to eke out the external evidence with astute deductions from the works.

Luigi Pirandello, 1867–1936, most of the time at least, wished to belong to the second category, and would have loved to have Matthew Arnold's words on Shakespeare applied to him: "Others abide our question, thou art free. / We ask and ask: Thou smilest and art still, / Out-topping knowledge."

If Pirandello authorized a biography by one F. V. Nardelli and contributed rather liberally to it, he did so less to amplify the narrative than to be the gray eminence behind it, and make sure the portrait remained grayly mysterious. If language can be a way of avoiding communication, biography can be a way of avoiding telling a large part of the biographical truth.

Gaspare Giudice's *Pirandello*, published twelve years ago in Turin, transferred the Maestro from the second category to the third: smashed the idol and revealed a man. Which is a very sad if commendable thing to do, especially when your subject was not always as commendable as he was sad. You had to admire Nardelli's Pirandello: the good artist was a good man. That Pirandello was a good artist is for Giudice a presupposition, but his conclusion, which pains him and must pain his readers, is that Pirandello the man was not good.

*Or seem to. Biographers have shown that Strindberg fantasized a lot.

Does it matter? Artists, after all, do not have to be saints or heroes. There is even a theory that they are amoral by rights, and many biographers have delighted to demonstrate that they were rascals. It is a question, though, whether the rascally geniuses have been anything like a majority, and there is no question that our greatest respect and affection are reserved for those geniuses who were also great men and preferably sages. If you are a mystery like Shakespeare, you can afford perhaps to leave it doubtful if you were a sage, which might explain why Pirandello wanted to be a mystery. Otherwise the supremely great—Dante, Milton, Goethe—are sages all, and one could even add to the list others who, while not uniformly sage, were still sages: Dostoyevski, Tolstoy, D. H. Lawrence, possibly Thomas Mann. When in his last years Brecht tried to join this august band, he was by the same token trying to become a sage. The doubt that many felt as to his sageness was indeed a doubt whether he belonged in such high company.

I don't think anyone can read Giudice's book and still believe Pirandello a sage. If his life has a lesson to teach, it is a lesson in folly. The story compels us to grapple with the problem of a magnificent artist who was a far from magnificent man. His own formula—"you either live or you write"—evades this issue. Pirandello did a lot of writing but as son, husband, father, and Platonic lover did as much living as any nonwriter. Or is the inner intent of his formula to say that being a writer of genius entitles you to live badly?

The blockbuster in Giudice's book is the chapter on Pirandello's fascism. It has been said that it was a fascism not to be taken seriously since it may have been motivated by the wish to squeeze money out of Mussolini. But since when was sycophancy the venial sin and fascism the mortal one? In any case, practically no one's fascism was just a doctrine out of a book. Nearly everyone's fascism was—like Pirandello's—a stance assumed opportunistically and feebly: some philosophy professor's bookish fascism might be almost admirable by comparison. The thing was that, in those days, nobody knew Mussolini was going to lose, so that only those with very pronounced convictions of a non-Fascist sort had any chance of escaping the plague.

Now almost the only really pronounced political convictions Pirandello ever expressed were Fascist opinions. Even his convictions about women and the family were not non-Fascist opinions. And the deeper question arises whether any of his convictions were more than playacting. Is anything in human life more than play-acting? That is the Pirandellian question par excellence, and it arose, in the first instance, because its author needed it to prove he was no worse than anyone else. Such is the modernist—that is, nihilist—application of old saws

92

about all the world's being a stage and all the men and women merely players. Giudice, in the Maestro's opinion, could by all means remove the Nardelli mask from Pirandello. What he would be uncovering, though, would only be a Giudice mask. The syllogism reads: No man has a face, Pirandello is a man, therefore Pirandello has no face.

Pirandello's fascism was "not serious," but whose was? Not even Mussolini's. Italy is not a "serious" country. What is sure is that Pirandello's fascism was fired, not by the idle promises of many quite good things which Mussolini made, but precisely by the antidemocratic bias and the brutal behavior. What first brought him enthusiastically in on the Fascist side was the murder of an anti-Fascist, Matteotti. What brought him to the point where he actually took political action of a sort—he had his 1934 Nobel Prize medal melted down to enrich the Italian government—was Mussolini's invasion of Abyssinia. What the Americans had done to the Indians, he explained in New York, the Italians were now doing to these Africans.

What is most horrifying is that Giudice shows fascism to have been an integral part of the life and personality of Pirandello. The rest of his book, if not equally horrifying, is no less dismaying than the chapter on fascism: there is so little to rejoice about in Pirandello's life except that he had talent. If this only meant he was miserable, we could offer compassion. We offer it anyway, but often wondering if we should. For one thing, Pirandello offered himself so much of it—self-pity anyway—and, for another, our compassion is monopolized at times by his victims. What emerges, if less from Giudice's own remarks than from quotations, is that anyone who came close to Pirandello was likely to become the victim, even that notoriously "insane wife" who, according to received Pirandello lore, was supposed to have victimized *him*. Giudice has reconstructed the story of the marriage from its inception. We used to be told that as a Sicilian, Pirandello in 1894 accepted an arranged marriage without cavil. Giudice shows that he had every opportunity to avoid it, and argues cogently that he must have accepted it for highly neurotic reasons.

The Pirandellian artist who does not live but writes does so because he is above mere living. The Pirandello whom Giudice presents is incapable of living out any of his primary relationships, and flees from all these challenges and responsibilities into writing. So far from being "above" the battle, he had his most creative period as a playwright—between 1916 and 1923—when the family battle raged most violently. Of that battle, though Giudice himself is content to use words like madness, there could be much more to say in this age of R. D. Laing, and especially that the wife's "madness" was definitely provoked by a family drama in which the protagonist was the husband. Pirandello's defense is never more, really, than that he was *not* sleeping with his daughter. Yet it seems fairly clear from the factual record that the daughter's attempt at suicide was not caused by the mother's "madness" alone. It is of collateral interest that Pirandello continued to address his daughter as a little girl when she was married and living in Chile.

For a serious gap in the story of Pirandello's last years, Giudice is not to blame. There has been quite a cover-up, to use the current term, of much of the Maestro's life all along the line, but no major episode has been so carefully concealed, or so it would seem, as the "love affair" with Marta Abba. Probably, as Mussolini himself seems to have dug out of the Maestro in conversation, it was not a love affair at all. Which again enabled Pirandello to pretend he was on to higher things; he considered Mussolini vulgar for interesting himself in lower things.* Yet no one has been able to get at the actual content of the relationship with Abba, though presumably we can learn something from the fact that Pirandello punished his daughter in his will in order to reward his mistress. Daughter and "mistress" then become implacable enemies.

These reflections of mine, it must be said, are based on the Italian edition of Giudice's book. The English edition, translated by Alastair Hamilton (Oxford University Press), is a rather dubious item. If you find the book in a library—without its dust jacket—you will be deceived into thinking it is complete. The dust jacket does mention abridgement in passing, but who would deduce that the Italian is about twice as long, much less that many of the changes are structural? The translator has not left out whole chapters, but has shortened very many paragraphs, and even sentences, throwing Giudice's style to the winds. Giudice for that matter could bring an even more serious charge against his *traduttore-traditore*, namely that the latter has omitted much of the evidence which validates the conclusions, conclusions without evidence being worthless.

One of the best things about Giudice's original is his intricate interweaving of internal with external evidence: the poems, novels, stories, and plays are constantly drawn on to fill out what is said of Pirandello's life. However sad, this life is fascinating. Giudice uses the work to bring out the fascination of the life, and the life to bring out the fascination of the work. Reasoning, I suppose, that non-Italians are unfa-

*See p. 84 above. The story was told to me by the late Corrado Alvaro.

miliar with the poems, novels, stories, and plays, the translator leaves out many of the quotations.

Did his publishers commission him to do all this? Even if they did not, they must take the responsibility. It seems to me that Pirandello is consistently sold short by publishers in England and America. Only part of his work has been brought out in English at all, and that part often in inadequate translations. Much that was published in English in Pirandello's lifetime has been allowed to out of print. These circumstances render the present action of the Oxford University Press doubly unfortunate. For, if this very great writer was a far from great man, this far from great man was a very great writer.

"THE THEATRE AGAINST ITSELF"?

Of books on theatre published in the last ten years, the one I have spent most hours with is probably *The Anti-Theatrical Prejudice* by Jonas Barish. Tracing a deeply felt and fiercely hostile attitude to theatre through Plato, Tertullian, Prynne, Rousseau, and Nietzsche, Mr. Barish goes on to locate traces of the prejudice—sometimes more than traces—in twentieth-century authors, the extreme case being Yvor Winters. But when, carried away by the momentum of an obviously strong argument, he goes so far as to group some of our finest playwrights under the heading "The Theatre against Itself," it is time, I think, to blow the whistle.

I will limit myself to Shaw, Brecht, and Pirandello. The first two were attacking a theatre that was itself untheatrical, if not always on the surface. On the surface it was offering nothing if not entertainment of a flamboyant ("theatrical") sort, but, below the surface, it was not providing that profound and accurate version of the truth which Shakespeare's "holding the mirror up to Nature" had established as the norm for serious drama. If Shaw and Brecht claimed to be giving a more "realistic" picture, they did not claim to be giving a more literal picture—rather, a more theatrical one, a picture devised with every theatrical resource at their command, all of these resources coming through their markedly and indeed extremely histrionic sensibility. Who more histrionic than Shaw—in life or on stage? The man was theatre personified. And if Brecht rejected the grand style of the Victorians and *la belle Epoque,* he did so in the name of what must be rated an *extreme* theatricalism: one that called attention to the boards of the theatre for what they have to offer in contrast to the anti-theatrical naturalists who asked us to ignore theatre and imagine what was on

97

stage was not in a theatre at all. What else is the famous Alienation Effect but a result of Brecht's insistence that we see not just the subject but the theatrical means by which it is defined—and by which, we can add, it becomes theatre?

> With Pirandello [Mr. Barish writes] commences a more disintegrating movement, a challenge to the theatre as an expressive medium, a rebuke to its age-old claim to be able to instruct us about our own true natures. . . . Pirandello reverses a basic premise of classical drama, the claim of the theatre to be an image of truth in which we can see our own lives mirrored. . . .

Yet, after several paragraphs of this, comes a "however":

> In the process, *however* [my italics], of subverting the customary claim, Pirandello paradoxically re-asserts it. For he shows us what our lives are like by showing that they bear little resemblance to the lessons we thought we had learned about them from the theatre of the older kind.

Back to Bernard Shaw: *Arms and the Man*, 1894. We thought we had learned from the earlier, "Victorian" plays what soldiering and chivalry were about. We here learn that "our" soldiers are not like that. Is this really a paradox? Shaw calls his correction of the earlier view Realism. By whatever name, it is couched in highly theatrical terms: a born man of the theatre here sets off theatrical fireworks to make his points. Brecht was to be grimmer in tone but no more disinclined to use ultra-theatrical means, as in the denouement of his *Threepenny Opera*. Delight in sheer theatrics is just as marked in both these writers as in Meyerbeer, Gilbert and Sullivan—or Mozart.

With Pirandello there might seem to be an initial problem. As a writer, in his earlier years, chiefly of verse and fiction, he shared, during those years, the literary man's contempt for theatrics and was consequently cautious in approaching that traditionally dreaded den of deceit the theatre. Mr. Barish is correct to observe that mistrust of actors as purveyors of a writer's meaning is carried over into *Six Characters*. He then concedes, perhaps a little shamefacedly, that Pirandello has a point, and manages to *show what our lives are like*—in other words does after all hold the mirror up to nature. But this Mr. Barish sees only in its negative aspect: "In Pirandellian theatre, *life* becomes the watery, inconstant, flickering reflection of what the *theatre* vainly tries to persuade us to see as final and unchanging. . . ."

There is a positive aspect. (It is the naturalistic theatre that is negative, that continually makes the point that everything majestic and large is a mirage, and that actuality is nasty and small. It uses a reducing mirror.) Pirandello used an enlarging mirror. Illusions? Yes. Illusions within illusions? Certainly. But not illusions of no account, illusions exclusively of scoundrels, fools, lunatics. The positivistic type of critic is impatient with Pirandello. Like the American middle-class public, he sees life as problems, and problems as having solutions. Pirandello has this in common with religious thinking (most of whose tenets he may have rejected) in that he saw life, not as soluble problems, but as inescapable predicaments—and sometimes as mysteries to which one owed a certain reverence or at least awe.

Now though a playwright cannot tangle with these topics as a metaphysician or a theologian might, he can dramatize, *theatricalize*, them, and I would propose a Pirandello who was not against any theatre save the one of the immediate past which he was endeavoring to transcend. At one time—the time of Shakespeare, the time of the Greeks—the theatre had confronted Mystery. In Ibsen, Strindberg, and Pirandello it does so again, as later, but I think in a smaller way, in Beckett and Pinter. All confront mystery theatrically—in the grand tradition of theatre—and we shall understand them better if we take note, point by point, how elements of theatre are brought to bear as they seek to send their beams of light into the enormous darkness.

If Mr. Barish insists, and I believe he does, on classifying writers as heroes or villains of the theatre, then Shaw, Brecht, and Pirandello should have been among his heroes. How has the art of theatre managed to survive at all into the era of modernism and the era of what is currently (however ineptly) called post-modernism? Through the work of Pirandello, I should think, more than any other single individual. It is certainly of interest that, in his later years, Pirandello lost his contempt for theatrics and in the process of creating his "trilogy of the theatre in the theatre" became a born-again theatricalist. Hinkfuss in the last play of this trilogy *(Tonight We Improvise)* is not just a negative account of a Reinhardt or Piscator but a positive account of the Man of the Theatre as against the Man of Letters: "It is we [the theatre people]," he says, "who give the work of art [its] life." In a preface published in the year he died, Pirandello finds an even crisper formulation of the thought: "In the theatre, a work of art is no longer the work of the author . . . but an act of life realized on stage from one moment to the next . . ."*

---

*I am drawing here on A. Richard Sogliuzzo's *Luigi Pirandello, Director,* in which (pp. 17–33) a whole trajectory is described from the 1908 essay, "Illustrators, Actors, and Translators," to the 1936 preface quoted above.

APPENDIX A: THE SOURCE OF RIGHT YOU ARE

"Here is a dream: in it I saw a deep courtyard with no exit, and from that frightening image Right You Are was born."* Between the dream and the play, however, came the short story, "Signora Frola and Signor Ponza, Her Son-in-Law."

Though the adapting of a story to the stage needs neither explanation nor apology, it is perhaps proper to observe that in Italy the relationship between stories (novelle) and plays has always been especially close and that, of Pirandello's forty-four plays, only ten are completely independent of his stories, and twenty-eight might correctly be described as adaptations.

The adaptations were not always improvements,** for while Pirandello regarded fiction as an elastic medium—a story could be any length, have any structure—in the dramatic realm he seemed to regard the three-act pattern as a Procrustes' bed. Even so successful a comedy as Right You Are raises questions, and those who consider it unsuccessful will doubtless prefer the story, their argument being as follows: "All that is essential in the play is in the story, which has something the play does not have, namely the device, beautifully handled, of a narrator who embodies the point of view of the town. The device by which Pirandello gets the townspeople into the play, on the other hand—bringing them onstage one after the other—is a clumsy one. And to get a point of view into the play, he has to invent a character, Laudisi, whose limitation is that he is the author's point of view incarnate. Not only is the

---

*See Almanacco Letterario Bompiani, 1938, as already cited above, p. 28.
**One critic, J. T. Paolantonacci, has seen the plays as a deformation, even a betrayal, of the stories (Le théâtre de Luigi Pirandello, Paris, n.d.).

play overextended vertically (too many characters, too much talk in each act), it is overextended horizontally—Acts Two and Three are redundant."

The fallacy in this argument is circular reasoning: only what is in the story is essential, therefore everything that is added in the play is inessential. Which is to overlook three points of principle. First, what was not essential to the shorter work may become essential to the longer; second, what is not essential to the story form may be essential to the dramatic form; third, an artistic element does not always have to be essential, it only has to be advantageous. If preference of the story is simply a preference of fiction to drama, there is nothing more to be said; far be it from a drama critic to pretend that an aisle seat in an auditorium is as cosy as an armchair at a fireside. But, contrariwise, if you are in an aisle seat, you will not bemoan the fact that a play lasts two hours instead of fifteen minutes like the story.

Though the expansion of a short story into a three-act play is a hazardous enterprise, it may be called successful if the three acts—however inessential parts of them may be to the original conception as we know it from the story—justify themselves as drama. It is no condemnation of Right You Are that it repeats things that in the story are stated only once; the question is whether, in their new context, the repetitions are effective or not. A question which would never have arisen had the play always been translated and performed lightly enough. Once it has the rhythm of farce, everyone would concede it the privileges of farce, chief of which, as was stressed above, is manic repetition.

And Right You Are is not merely longer than the story, and more philosophical, it is also much larger emotionally and spiritually. When Ponza and Frola are no longer reported on by a third person but are allowed to speak for themselves, they acquire a stature the story never approaches. To some extent, this is the result of transference to the dramatic medium as such; for the small characters of naturalism, to pass from the pages of a storybook to the boards of a stage is a sort of promotion. The "little man," who is such a worm in modern fiction, is quite a bulldog in Death of a Salesman; for in the theatre he has to speak for himself, and he has the actor to help him. This is not to say that the change from narrative to drama has done Pirandello's work for him and that the actors will do the rest. To changes that are automatic he adds others that require a genius for dramatic composition. In place of the attractive solo which is the story he does the larger job of orchestration which a play imposes: Laudisi, the "crowd," and the Ponza-Frola trio have to be combined like woodwinds, brass, and strings. And if a novelist's characters have something a playwright's do not, and the latter's need the actors to fill them out, the playwright's characters have something the novelist's do not: they are not only characters but roles. Ponza and Frola are interesting characters in both story and play; in the play they are also great parts.

In noting the differences between the story "Signora Frola" and the play Right You Are, it would be foolish to overlook the resemblances. I have so far spoken as if the story, by contrast with the play, were of an accepted sort, yet, in fact, it must seem just as eccentric in the history of fiction as the play is in the history of drama. An Italian critic has defined Pirandello's position in the evolution of narrative art in these words:

> The novella rests no longer on a fact but on a trovata (trouvaille, brain-storm, conceit), no longer on a character-study but on the presentation of a maschera (theatrical archetype). Hence the narrative is broken, convulsed, turbulent, and the interest is not in the unfolding of the action, but in separating out the moments on which the light has to be concentrated.*

What interests the critic of fiction is that this kind of story leads away from the main tradition of narrative. What interests the drama critic is that it leads to the theatre which is the proper place for concentrated light, big moments, and turbulent action. The two greatest of Pirandello's trouvailles are, first, the idea of characters coming onstage in search of their author and, second, the idea of a masker fixed in his masquerade for life and building the eleventh century in the twentieth: both ideas are theatrical in more than a figurative sense. And what is a trouvaille after all but a coup de théâtre?

SIGNORA FROLA AND SIGNOR PONZA, HER SON-IN-LAW**

You see that, don't you? It's enough to drive everyone right out of their minds, not to be able to figure which of them is mad, this Signora Frola or this Signor Ponza, her son-in-law. Such things happen only in Valdana. The unhappy town is a magnet for every sort of crackpot.

Either she's mad or he's mad, there's nothing else for it, one of the two *must* be mad. For it's a matter of nothing less than . . . but it's best if I begin at the beginning.

---

*Giuseppe Petronio in his booklet *Pirandello novelliere e la crisi del realismo* (Lucca, 1950).

**This translation is based on "La signora Frola e il signor Ponza, suo genero" in *Novelle per un anno*, 3d ed., Vol. II (Milan: Arnoldo Mondadori Editore, 1940). The writing of the story is conjecturally dated as 1915 by Pirandello's official bibliographer. The story has appeared in English as "A Mother-in-Law" in *The Medals and Other Stories* (New York: E. P. Dutton, 1939) and as "Mrs. Frola and Her Son-in-Law, Mr. Ponza" in Luigi Pirandello, *Quattro novelle*, trans. by V. M. Jeffrey ("Harrap's Bilingual Series" [London: Harrap, 1939]).

I'm terribly concerned, I can tell you, at the distress that has been the lot of every Valdanian for the past three months—it's not Signora Frola and Signor Ponza I'm worried about. It may be true that a great misfortune has befallen these two individuals, but it's also true that it's driven at least one of them mad and that he—or she—has been so helped out by the other that you just can't figure, as I said, which of the two it is that's mad. Now these people may know the best way of consoling each other, but what are they doing to our town? How *can* they? They make it impossible to judge—one way or the other. You can't tell fantasy from reality any more. It's agony, it's appalling, and it doesn't stop: every day we see those two before us, look them in the face, know that one of them's mad, study and scrutinize them, examine them from head to foot—in vain! It's impossible to find out which is which! To find out where fantasy begins, where reality leaves off! And the dangerous notion naturally arises that it's six of one and half a dozen of the other—that any reality can quite well be a fantasy—or vice versa! Think of that!! If I were in the Governor's shoes, for the good of the people of Valdana I wouldn't hesitate to expel Signora Frola and Signor Ponza from our town!!!

But let's begin at the beginning.

This Signor Ponza came to Valdana three months ago as an executive secretary in the Government Building. He went to live in that new tenement on the edge of town—the one they call the Beehive. Over there. A tiny apartment on the top floor. It has three sad old windows on the other side, looking out over the countryside—the northern façade, facing all those pale orchards, has got in a sad way indeed, no one knows why, for it isn't old—and three windows on this side, in the courtyard ringed by the railing of a balcony divided into sections by an iron grill. On this railing, way up high, hang many baskets, all ready to be lowered at need on a rope.

At the same time, however, and to the astonishment of all, this Signor Ponza rented another small apartment, three rooms and kitchen, in the center of town—to be precise, Via dei Santi, Number 15. He said it was for his mother-in-law, Signora Frola. And in fact she arrived five or six days later. And Signor Ponza went to meet her at the station—went quite alone—took her to her new home and left her there alone.

Now of course we all understand it if a daughter gets married and leaves her mother's house to go and live with her husband—in another city if necessary. But if the mother can't bear being away from her daughter and leaves her house and her home town and follows her and then, in a city where she and her daughter are both strangers, goes and lives on her own—*that* we don't understand, unless we assume that husband and mother-in-law are so incompatible there can be no living together even in these circumstances.

Naturally, this is what everyone thought. And the loser in the general esteem was of course Signor Ponza. If anyone suggested that—in lack of sympathy perhaps, or sheer intolerance—Signora Frola must bear a small part of the blame, everyone else cited the maternal love that must be drawing her toward her daughter—and she not allowed to be with her.

It must be admitted that the appearance of the couple played a great part in arousing this general sympathy for Signora Frola and in creating the impression of Signor Ponza that suddenly took hold of everyone—namely, that he was a hard, and even a cruel, man. Thickset, neckless, swarthy as an African, with abundant and shaggy hair above a low forehead, thick, bristling eyebrows that join in the middle, the big sleek moustaches of a policeman, and in the dark, fixed eyes with almost no whites to them a violent and exasperated intensity that he only with difficulty controls, an intensity that could either be that of somber grief or that of contempt for others—Signor Ponza is certainly not the man to induce sympathy or confidence. Signora Frola, on the other hand, is a pale and delicate old lady of fine, indeed most noble, features. Her melancholy, though real, is not ponderous but sweet and airy. It doesn't stop her being very affable with everybody.

Now no sooner had Signora Frola given proof of the affability that was so natural in her than the general aversion to Signor Ponza increased; for the old lady's nature revealed itself to all as not only gentle, forgiving, tolerant, but also full of indulgent sympathy for the harm her son-in-law does her. And it was discovered that Signor Ponza not only kept the poor mother in a separate house, he carried his cruelty to the extent of forbidding her the very sight of her daughter.

"Not cruelty, not cruelty!" Signora Frola at once protests on her visits to the ladies of Valdana. And she extends her small hands, deeply disturbed that this can have been thought of her son-in-law. And she hastens to extol all his virtues, to say all the good about him that you could possibly imagine: what loving care he shows, how much consideration—not toward her daughter only but also toward her, yes, toward her, he is most attentive, selfless, oh, not cruel, no, for pity's sake! It's simply this: he wants his little wife all, all to himself, that's what Signor Ponza wants, he admits that she loves her mother, he gladly admits it, but he wants her love to come to the old lady indirectly, through him, *he* wants to bring it to her. Yes, it may look like cruelty, she sees that, but it isn't, it's something else, something that she, Signora Frola, understands perfectly but has difficulty putting into words. His nature, that's it—or rather, no, maybe it's a kind of illness, how can she put it? *Dio mio*, just look at his eyes, that'll settle it. Maybe they give a bad impression at first, those eyes, but to someone like herself who knows how to read them, they say everything, they tell of the fullness of the love in him, a closed world of love in which his wife is to live, she must never go out, and no one else come in, not even her mother. Jealousy? Yes, perhaps, if such a common word could sum up a love so total, so exclusive.

Selfishness? Yet a selfishness which gives itself utterly and provides a world to live in—for his own wife! After all, the selfishness would be her own if she tried to force her way into this closed world of love, to try and get in by force when her daughter is happy. Happy and adored. To a mother, that should be enough. For the rest, it's not true that she doesn't see her daughter. She sees her two or three times a day. She enters the courtyard of the house. She rings the bell and at once her daughter comes to the balcony above. "How are you, Tildina?" "Very well, Mother, what about you?" "As God wills, my daughter. Let the basket down!" And in the basket are always a few words by way of a letter with the day's news. That's all, and isn't it enough? That's how it's been for four years, and Signora Frola has got used to it. She's resigned to it, yes. It doesn't hurt her now.

It is easy to understand how this resignation of Signora Frola's, the way she says she got used to her own suffering, should—shall I say?—redound to the discredit of Signor Ponza, her son-in-law. And her working herself up into lengthy apologies only makes things worse.

It is therefore with real indignation—and I will also say with fear—that the ladies of Valdana, after Signora Frola's first visit, receive on the following day the announcement of another unexpected visit—from Signor Ponza, who begs them to see him for but two minutes if it isn't too inconvenient: he has a "declaration" to make which is "a matter of duty."

With burning cheeks, almost choking, his eyes harder and more dismal than ever, in his hand a handkerchief whose whiteness, along with that of his shirt cuffs and collar, is in appalling contrast with the darkness of his complexion, hair, and suit, continually wiping off the sweat that drips from his low forehead and from the violet rash of his face, a sweat that proceeds not from heat but from the obvious pressure of the violence he is doing himself (his long hands with their long nails are trembling too), Signor Ponza confronts the terrified eyes of the ladies in that same drawing room and asks if his mother-in-law, Signora Frola, paid them a visit on the previous day and if—here he speaks with an effort, with ever growing agitation—if she spoke of her daughter and if she said he absolutely forbids her to see her and to go up to her apartment.

Seeing him so agitated, the ladies (as may easily be believed) hasten to reply that, well, yes, Signora Frola did speak of his forbidding her to see her daughter but that she also said all the good about him that anyone could possibly imagine, excusing him for that prohibition, clearing him of every trace of blame.

But instead of being quieted by the ladies' replies, Signor Ponza gets more agitated than ever, his eyes harder, more fixed, more dismal, the large drops of sweat more frequent; and so, eventually, with a still more violent effort to control himself, he comes to the "declaration" which is a "matter of duty."

Which is simply this: Signora Frola, poor woman, though she doesn't *seem* mad, *is* mad.

She's been mad for four years, yes. And her madness consists precisely in believing that he doesn't wish to have her see her daughter. What daughter? She is dead. Her daughter died four years ago. And Signora Frola went mad from grief at her death. Better so, for madness was her escape from this grief. After all it was the only way she *could* escape it—to believe it isn't true her daughter is dead but that he, her son-in-law, refuses to let her see her.

In charity toward an unfortunate—as a duty, in fact—he, Signor Ponza, has been humoring her in her pitiful folly for four years, making many heavy sacrifices along the way: he maintains two households which cost him almost more than he can pay, one for himself, and one for her, and he obliges his second wife who, luckily, complies willingly in the spirit of charity, to help humor the old lady too. But there are limits even to charity, to duty, aren't there? If only in his capacity as a public official, Signor Ponza cannot allow the town to believe this cruel and improbable thing—that he would forbid a poor mother to see her own daughter—out of jealousy or anything else.

His declaration made, Signor Ponza bows to the astonished ladies and goes away. But before the ladies' astonishment has had time to subside a little, Signora Frola is here again with her sweet and airy melancholy asking to be excused if, because of her, the good ladies had suffered any shock at the visit of Signor Ponza, her son-in-law.

And Signora Frola, with the greatest simplicity and naturalness in the world, herself makes a declaration—but in confidence, for pity's sake! because Signor Ponza is a public official, and that's why he didn't speak out the first time, don't you see? Because his career might be seriously affected. Signor Ponza, poor man—as secretary in the Government Building above reproach, efficient, correct in all his actions, in all his thoughts, a man simply full of good qualities—Signor Ponza, poor man, is—on this one point—not reasonable. Poor man, it's *he* that's mad. And his madness consists precisely in this: he believes that his wife died four years ago and goes about saying that *she*, Signora Frola, is the mad one because she thinks her daughter still alive. No, he doesn't say this to justify his almost maniacal jealousy and the prohibition against seeing her daughter, no, poor man, he believes, seriously believes, that his wife is dead and that this present wife is his second. A sad story indeed! Loving his delicate little wife all too much, this man had come near destroying her, killing her—they had had to take her away from him in secret and shut her up in a sanitarium without his knowledge. Well, the unhappy fellow, whose head had already been turned badly enough by that frenzy of love, went quite mad. He believed that his wife was really dead. And the idea fixed itself in his head till he couldn't get rid of it, even when, about a year later, his wife, in the best of health again, was brought back to him. He believed it was someone else. His friends and relations had to get together and go through the pretense of a second wedding. This completely restored his mental equilibrium.

By this time Signora Frola believes she has reason to suspect that her son-in-law has been entirely sane for a while and is pretending, only pretending to believe this wife is his second, so he can keep her all to himself, out of contact with everybody, for perhaps, in spite of everything, the fear flashes across his mind that his wife could be taken from him in secret again.

Yes. Or how could you explain the way he takes care of her, the mother-in-law, all the attention he gives her—if he really believes he now has a second wife? He wouldn't feel himself under such an obligation toward one who actually wasn't his mother-in-law any longer— now would he? Signora Frola says this, mind you, not as further evidence that he is the mad one but to prove to herself that her suspicion is well founded.

"Meanwhile," she concludes with a sigh that takes the form, on her lips, of a sweet and most mournful smile, "meanwhile the poor girl must pretend she is not herself but someone else. And I must pretend I am mad and believe my daughter still alive. It isn't very hard, thank God, because she is there, my daughter is healthy and full of life, I see her, I talk to her, but I am condemned not to live with her, I must see her and talk with her from a distance, so that he can believe, or pretend to believe, that my daughter, God forbid, is dead and that this wife is his second. But I say again, what does it matter if in this way we succeed in bringing peace to both of them? I know my daughter is adored and happy, I see her, I speak to her, and for love of her—and him—I'm resigned to living like this and being thought mad. We must be patient, Signora. . . ."

Now: don't you have the impression that we all have our mouths agape and our eyes popping out of our heads? That the whole town of Valdana is out of its senses? Which of the two to believe? Which of them is mad? Where does reality leave off? And fantasy begin?

Signor Ponza's wife could tell. But she is not to be trusted if she says she's his second wife—in front of him. Nor is she to be trusted if she says she's Signora Frola's daughter—in front of her. One would have to take her to one side and have her speak the truth confidentially. Impossible. Mad or not mad, Signor Ponza really *is* jealous and won't let anyone see his wife. He keeps her up there under lock and key as in a prison, and the fact undoubtedly favors Signora Frola, but Signor Ponza says he is forced to act this way, and in fact that his wife insists on it, for fear that Signora Frola should unexpectedly drop in on her. It could be a pretext. There is also the fact that Signor Ponza doesn't even keep a maid. He says this is just to economize—he has to pay the rent on two households. And he himself does the daily shopping. And the wife who, according to him, is not the daughter of Signora Frola, in compassion for the poor old creature who was once her husband's mother-in-law, does all the housework, even the lowest drudgery, without recourse to a maid. It seems a bit much. But it's also true that this state of affairs can be explained, if not as compassion on her part, as jealousy on his.

Meanwhile Signor Ponza's declaration has satisfied the governor of the province. But Ponza's appearance is not in his favor, nor is a great deal of his conduct—in the eyes of the ladies of Valdana, who are all more inclined to believe Signora Frola. The latter has been most anxious to show them the affectionate messages her daughter has let down in the basket and many other private documents. Signor Ponza destroys their value as evidence, however, by saying that they have all been written just to bolster the pitiful deception.

At any rate, this much is certain: that the two of them show, the one for the other, a marvellous spirit of self-sacrifice that is most touching; each shows for the (assumed) madness of the other the most exquisitely compassionate consideration. Each of them argues with the sweetest reasonableness; in fact no one at Valdana would ever have dreamed of saying either of them was mad if they hadn't said it themselves—Signor Ponza of Signora Frola, Signora Frola of Signor Ponza.

Often Signora Frola goes to see her son-in-law in the Government Building to ask his advice about something. Or she awaits him at the end of the day to go and buy something with him. For his part, every evening and very often in a free hour during the day, Signor Ponza goes to see Signora Frola in her furnished apartment. Whenever they meet on the street by accident, they proceed together with the utmost friendliness. He politely walks at her left, and, if she is tired, offers her his arm. And they walk on together—amid the anger or amazement or distress of the people who study and scrutinize them, examine them from head to foot—in vain! They are still totally unable to comprehend which of the two is mad, where fantasy begins, where reality leaves off.

APPENDIX B: BIBLIOGRAPHICAL NOTES

1. Bentley translations of Pirandello.

Liolà. In *Naked Masks*, ed. Bentley. E. P. Dutton, 1952. (Many people have assumed that all the translations in this standard collection, still in print in 1986, are by Bentley. But, though Bentley has made translations of *Six Characters*, *Enrico IV*, and *Right You Are*, he has been prevented by the Dutton company from including these items in *Naked Masks*, presumably because they owned the faulty, older translations and no longer had to pay anything for their use.)

Right You Are. Columbia University Press, 1954. (This volume also contains the story on which *Right You Are* is based. The play was reprinted in the Bentley anthology *The Great Playwrights*. Doubleday, 1970.)

The Man with the Flower in His Mouth. In *Tulane Drama Review,* June 1957. (Reprinted in the Samuel Moon anthology *One Act.* Grove Press, 1961.)

The Emperor (Enrico IV). In *The Genius of the Italian Theatre*, ed. Bentley. New American Library, 1964. (Reprinted in the Nobel Prize Library. Helvetica Press, 1971.)

Six Characters in Search of an Author. In *The Great Playwrights*. Doubleday, 1970. (Reprinted in the Nobel Prize Library. Helvetica Press, 1971. The Bentley translation of the Preface had already appeared in *Naked Masks*, 1952.)

2. Bentley commentary on Pirandello not in this book.

"Appendix II: Biographical and Historical." *Naked Masks*, 1952.

"We Need Pirandello Today." In *Theatre Arts*, May 1952.

Notes in the Columbia edition of *Right You Are*, 1954.

"A Director's Theatre." In *What Is Theatre?* Horizon Press, Beacon Press, 1956. Reprinted by Proscenium Press, 1984.

"Pirandello, Luigi." In Gassner and Quinn, *Reader's Encyclopedia of World*

Drama. Thomas Y. Crowell, 1969. (But this overlaps with the "Life and Works" essay in the present book.)

3. Earlier publications of material in this book.

"Pirandello and Modern Comedy." First published in the *Rocky Mountain Review,* Winter 1946; reprinted that same year in *The Playwright as Thinker.*

"Liolà and Other Plays" was originally the introduction to the Pirandello volume *Naked Masks* (1952), then was reprinted as a chapter of *In Search of Theatre* (1953).

"Right You Are" was originally the introduction to a separate edition of the play of that name (1954), then was reprinted in *Theatre of War* (1972).

"From *The Life of the Drama*" is just that (1964).

"Enrico IV." First published in the *Tulane Drama Review,* Spring 1966; reprinted in *The Great Playwrights* (1970) and *Theatre of War* (1972).

"Six Characters in Search of an Author" First published as a booklet by the Istituto di Cultura Italiana of New York (1968); reprinted in *Drama Review,* Fall 1968, *The Great Playwrights* (1970), and *Theatre of War* (1972).

"The Life and Works of Luigi Pirandello" was the essay on Pirandello in the Nobel Prize Library (1971).

"Gaspare Giudice's Biography" is a review from *The Village Voice,* July 21, 1975.

"Appendix A: The Source of *Right You Are*" was originally the appendix to the separate edition of *Right You Are* (1954).

4. Since Naked Masks

Naked Masks contains a Pirandello bibliography as of 1952. A vast Pirandello literature has accumulated since then. Books on Pirandello which the author has found interesting and/or useful include:

Alonge, Roberto. *Pirandello tra realismo e mistificazione.* Naples: Guida Editori, 1972.

Bassnett-McGuire, Susan. *Pirandello.* New York: Grove Press, 1983.

Bishop, Tom. *Pirandello and the French Theater.* New York: New York University Press, 1960.

Cambon, Glauco, ed. *Pirandello: A Collection of Essays.* Englewood Cliffs, N.J.: Spectrum Books, 1967.

Giudice, Gaspare. *Pirandello: A Biography.* New York: Oxford University Press, 1975.

Oliver, Roger W. *Dreams of Passion.* New York: New York University Press, 1979.

Paolucci, Anne. *Pirandello's Theater.* Edwardsville: Southern Illinois University Press, 1974.

Rauhut, Franz. *Der junge Pirandello oder das Werden eines existentiellen Geistes.* Munich: Beck, 1964.

Sogliuzzo, A. Richard. *Luigi Pirandello, Director: The Playwright in the Theatre*. Metuchen, N.J.: Scarecrow Press, 1982.

Those interested in the widely differing perspectives from which this author of differing perspectives may be viewed should not miss "Pirandello and Humor," in *The Worm of Consciousness* by Nicola Chiaromonte (New York: Harcourt Brace Jovanovich, 1976), or "Pirandello: A Work in Progress," in *Theatrewritings* by Bonnie Marranca (New York: PAJ Publications, 1984). Different again is the chapter on Pirandello in Maurice Valency's *The End of the World* (New York: Oxford University Press, 1980).

Since *Naked Masks*, which itself contains the Preface to *Six Characters*, some of Pirandello's theoretical work has appeared in English, notably excerpts from his book-length essay on humor in the *Massachusetts Review*, Spring 1965, and *Tulane Drama Review*, Spring 1966, plus the following complete essays:

"Theatre and Literature," trans. A. M. Webb, and "The New Theatre and the Old," trans. Herbert Goldstone. In *The Creative Vision*, ed. Block and Salinger. New York: Grove Press, 1960.

"The Italian Theatre," trans. Anne Paolucci. In *The Genius of the Italian Theatre*. New American Library, 1964.

"Spoken Action," trans. Fabrizio Melano, and "Eleanora Duse," trans. anonymous. In *The Theory of the Modern Stage*, ed. Eric Bentley. London: Penguin, 1968.

(Related material not mentioned in *Naked Masks* had appeared in English even before 1952, notably, "Pirandello Distills Shaw," *New York Times*, January 13, 1924 [to be reprinted later in Eric Bentley's *The Great Playwrights*, vol. 2, Doubleday, 1970]; and "Tendencies of the Modern Novel," *Fortnightly Review* [April 1934].)

INDEX

INDEX TO PIRANDELLO WORKS AND
   CHARACTERS

About Either One or No One, 82
Agazzi, 31, 32, 33
All for the Best, 19, 22, 81
Amalia, 32
As You Desire Me, 82, 84
Aunt Croce, 13
Aunt Gesa, 15

Baldovino, 12
Belcredi, 47, 48, 49, 50, 51, 53, 55, 56, 89
Berecche and the War, 81
Boy, 63
But It's Not Serious, 81

Cap and Bells, 34, 81
Carnival of the Dead, The, 81
Centuri, 33
Ciampa, 34
Cini, Signora, 29, 31
Ciuzza, 15
"Conversations with Characters," 60n, 85

Delia Morello, 17, 18
Diana and Tuda, 82, 84
Diego Cinci, 34
Dina, 32
Director, 64, 69–71, 72, 73, 74, 76, 77, 86
Doctor Genoni, 43–44, 47, 50, 53, 56, 72

Each in His Own Way, 16, 18, 19, 34, 82
Enrico IV: *see* Henry IV
Enrico IV, xii, 16, 19, 37, 43–56, 59, 66, 72, 81–
   82, 86–90
Epilogue, The, 81

Father, 18, 40, 59, 60, 61, 62, 63, 64–67, 69–75
Frida, 44, 49, 51
Frola, Signora, 2, 17, 28–29, 33, 35, 38, 65,
   102

Game of Role Playing, The, 81, 86
Giants of the Mountain, 82
giara e altre novelle, La, 75n
Giovanni, 45, 54
Governor, 33
Grass in Our Garden, 81

Henry IV, 12, 17, 43–46, 48, 49–53, 54, 55, 56,
   65, 66, 87, 88, 89
Her Husband, 80
Hinkfuss, 99
Horse in the Moon, A, 81
"Humor" ("L'umorismo"), 9, 13, 28

If Not Thus, 81
"Illustrators, Actors, and Translators," 99n

Jests of Death and Life, 81

Landolf, 45
Late Mattia Pascal, The, 80, 85

Laudisi, 1, 7, 17, 25, 26, 27, 28–30, 31, 33, 34, 74, 101, 102
Lazarus, 82
Life I Gave You, The, 21, 22, 82
Like the First Time Only Better, 81
Liolà, 11–12, 14, 15, 16, 17
Liolà, 10–15, 16, 17, 18, 21
Loves Without Love, 81
Luzza, 15

Madama Pace, 28, 59, 60n, 66–67, 68, 69, 71, 73, 74, 85
Man, Beast, and Virtue, 19, 81
Matilda, Countess, 44, 45–46, 47, 48, 49, 50–51, 55, 56, 88, 89
Medals and Other Stories, The, 103n
Merry Go Round, The, 80
Mita, 12–14
Mommina, 17
Mother, 66, 71
"Mother-in-Law, A," 103n
"Mrs. Frola and Her Son-in-Law, Mr. Ponza," 103n
Mrs. Morley One and Two, 81

Naked Life, 81
Naked Masks (Maschere nude), 34
Nela, 15
Nenni, Signora, 29, 31
New Colony, The, 82
No One Knows How, 82
Novelle per un anno, 103n

Old and the Young, The, 80
One, None, and a Hundred Thousand, 80
Outcast, The, 80

Pleasure of Honesty, The, 12, 19, 81
Ponza, 2, 16, 17, 28–29, 30, 33, 34, 35, 38, 65, 102
Ponza, Signora, 29
Prestino, 34

Quattro novelle, 103n

Rhenish Elegies, 49
Right You Are [Così è (se vi pare)], 1–2, 3–4, 5, 6–7, 15–16, 17, 18, 21, 25–35, 37–38, 40, 56, 65, 72, 81, 89, 101–3

Shoot, 80
"Signora Frola and Signor Ponza, Her Son-in-Law" ("La signora Frola e il signor Ponza, suo genero"), 101–10
Sirelli, 29, 31, 33
Sirelli, Signora, 31
Six Characters in Search of an Author (Sei personaggi in cerca d'autore), xii, 5, 10n, 16, 17, 18, 19, 28, 33, 37, 40, 41–42, 57–77, 81, 82, 85–86, 89, 98
Son, 62, 63, 67
Stepdaughter, 18, 60, 61, 64, 66, 69, 70, 71, 73, 76

Think of That, Giacomino!, 81
To Clothe the Naked, 5, 34, 82
To Find Oneself, 82, 84
Tomorrow Is Monday, 81
Tonight We Improvise, 16, 41, 82, 99
Tony, 56
"Tragedy of a Character," 60n, 85
Trap, The, 81
Trios, 81
Tuzza, 12–13, 17
Two-faced Erma, 81
Two Masks, The, 81

Uncle Simone, 12–13

Vise, The, 81

When I Was Crazy, 81
When One Is Somebody, 82
Wives' Friend, The, 82, 84

INDEX TO GENERAL SUBJECTS

Abba, Marta, 83, 84, 94
Adalbert (Bishop of Bremen), 56, 88
Adelaide, 44, 45, 87
Aesop, 25
Agnes, 44, 45, 88
Allgemeine Geschichte, 45
Almanacco Letterario Bompiani, 28n, 101n
Alvaro, Corrado, 94
Anti-Theatrical Prejudice, The, 97
Antigone, 27
Antony and Cleopatra, 72
Aristophanes, 1

Aristotle, xi, 58, 71, 73
Arms and the Man, 98
Arnold, Matthew, 39, 91
Augustine, St., 90

Barish, Jonas, 97–99
Becker, Ernest, 89
Beckett, Samuel, 56, 99
Behrman, S. N., 1
Berkeley, George, 12, 26
Bernstein, Henry, 1
Bertha, 44, 45, 87
Betrayal of the Body, 89
Bismarck, Otto, Prince von, 87
Bolero, 29
Bontempelli, Massimo, 20, 35
Brecht, Bertolt, xi, 29, 92, 97–98, 99
Brustein, Robert, 58n

Calderón de la Barca, Pedro, 70
Cavalleria rusticana, 11
Chaplin, Sir Charles, 6
Charley's Aunt, 85
Chekhov, Anton, 30
Chiarelli, Luigi, 1, 4
Crémieux, Benjamin, 45, 87
Cyrano de Bergerac, 7

Damiani, Peter (St. Peter Damian), 45, 88
D'Annunzio, Gabriele, 21
Dante, 84, 87, 92
Daumier, Honoré, 31
Dead City, The, 21
Death of a Salesman, 102
Debenedetti, Giacomo, 19, 20–21
Denial of Death, The, 89
Divided Self, The, 65, 89
Dostoyevski, Feodor, 55, 92
"Dover Beach," 39
Drama Review, 83n
Drury, F. K. W., 58n
Dullin, Charles, 31
Dumas, Alexandre (the Younger), 1
Duse, Eleanora, 10n

Edward VIII, 85
Einstein, Albert, 85
Electra, 55
Empedocles, 9n, 10

Emperor Jones, The, 29
Enemy of the People, An, 15
Essays in Modern Italian Literature, 86
Esslin, Martin, 85

finzioni dell'anima, Le, 10n
Fliess, Wilhelm, 61n
Freud, Sigmund, xi, 61, 65, 67, 73

Games People Play, 86
Garbo, Greta, 82
Garibaldi, Giuseppe, 79
Gay, John, 29
Gentile, Giovanni, 75, 77n
Ghosts, 58
Gielgud, Sir John, 31
Gilbert, Sir William Schwenck, 98
Giraudoux, Jean, 55
Giudice, Gaspare, 82, 83, 91–95
Goethe, Johann Wolfgang von, xii, 92
Goffman, Erving, 39
Gorgias, 10
Gramatica, Emma, 21, 22
gran teatro del mundo, El, 70
Green Cockatoo, The, 10n
Gregory VII, Pope, 45, 46, 55, 87, 88
Gustav Mahler and the Courage to Be, 89

Hamilton, Alastair, 94
Hamlet, xii, 49, 54, 59, 72, 89
Hanno (Bishop of Cologne), 88
Hart, Bernard, 88
Hauptmann, Gerhart, 1
Hedda Gabler, 89
Henry (Bishop of Augsburg), 45, 88
Henry IV (of the Holy Roman Empire), 43, 44, 45, 46, 48, 49, 52, 53, 55, 87–88, 89
Hofmannsthal, Hugo von, 10n
Holbrook, David, 89

Ibsen, Henrik, 1, 9, 19–20, 34, 37, 38, 46, 58, 59, 65, 99
Interpretation of Dreams, The, 61n

James, William, 85, 90
Jeffrey, V. M., 103n
Jonson, Ben, 50
Journal of the American Psychoanalytic Association, 62n

Kafka, Franz, 3, 4, 6
Kant, Immanuel, 87
Kierkegaard, Søren, 75
King Lear, 40
Kligerman, Charles, 62–63, 64, 73, 89
Kott, Jan, 49
Krutch, Joseph Wood, 58n

Laing, R. D., 65, 66, 89, 93
Lanza, Giuseppe, 75n
Lawrence, D. H., 92
Ledoux, Fernand, 30
Life and Opinions of Tristram Shandy, The, xii
Life of the Drama, The, xi
Lifton, Robert Jay, 86
Lina (cousin), 79, 80, 84
Living Age, 83n
Livingston, Arthur, 86
Lo Vecchio Musti, Manlio, 83
Lowen, Alexander, 89
Luigi Pirandello, Director, 99n

Mann, Thomas, 92
Mantle, Burns, 58n
Manzoni, Alessandro, 86n
Marcel, Gabriel, 40
Marchesini, Giovanni, 10n
Markey, Gene, 82
Martoglio, Nino, 81
Marzocco, Il, 26n
Mask and the Face, The, 1
Matilda of Tuscany, 44, 45, 46, 49, 87, 88
Matteotti, Giacomo, 83, 93
Maugham, W. Somerset, 1
Meyerbeer, Giacomo, 98
Milton, John, 92
Minkowski, E., 65
Molière, 26, 29, 50
Mozart, W. A., 98
Mussolini, Benito, 39, 75, 82, 83, 84, 92, 93, 94

Nardelli, F. V., 85, 91, 93
Nathan, George Jean, 2, 7
Negri, Gaetano, 10n
New York Times, The, 85
Nietzsche, Friedrich, 97

Ojetti, Ugo, 26n
Oncken, Wilhelm, 45
O'Neill, Eugene, 29

Paolantonacci, J. T., 101n
Pascal, Blaise, 9n, 10
Petronio, Giuseppe, 103n
Pictorial Review, 83n
Pills of Hercules, The, 1
Pinter, Harold, 99
Pirandello, Fausto, 80
Pirandello, Lietta, 80, 82, 94
Pirandello, Maria Antonietta, 38, 80, 82–83, 84, 93–94
Pirandello, Stefano, 60n, 80, 82, 85
Pirandello: A Biography, 91–95
Pirandello novelliere e la crisi del realismo, 103n
Piscator, Erwin, 99
Plato, 42, 97
Poetics, xi
Polakov, Lester, 32
Politics of Experience, The, 65n
Portulano, Maria Antonietta: *see* Pirandello, Maria Antonietta
preparazione, La, xii
Presentation of Self in Everyday Life, The, 39
Proust, Marcel, 6
Prynne, William, 97
"Psychoanalytic Study of Pirandello's *Six Characters in Search of an Author*, A," 62n, 89
Psychology of Insanity, The, 88
Puss in Boots, 10n

Quadrivio, 83n

Rauhut, Franz, 10n
Ravel, Maurice, 29
Reinhardt, Max, 99
Revue de Paris, 77n
Rostand, Edmond, 1, 7
Rousseau, Jean Jacques, 97
Royce, Josiah, 26
Ruggeri, Ruggero, 22

Saggi critici, 21n
Santayana, George, 40, 41
Sartre, Jean-Paul, 28
Schnitzler, Arthur, 10n
Schulz-Lander, Jenny, 84
Segni dei tempi, 10n
Shakespeare, William, xii, 72, 91, 92, 97, 99
Shavian, The, 77n
Shaw, Bernard, 1, 3, 9, 19, 37, 77, 81, 97–98, 99

Simmel, Georg, 22n
Sogliuzzo, A. Richard, 99n
Stanislavsky, Konstantin, 21, 30
Stendhal, 14
Strachey, James, 61n
Strindberg, August, 1, 3, 61, 91, 99
Studi sul teatro contemporaneo, 9, 20n
Suetonius, 64n
Sullivan, Sir Arthur, 98

"Teatro di Luigi Pirandello, Il," 9
Tertullian, 97
théâtre de Luigi Pirandello, Le, 101n
Theory of Mind as Pure Act, The, 75n
Threepenny Opera, The, 98
Through the Looking Glass, 26
Tieck, Ludwig, 10n

Tilgher, Adriano, 9, 19, 20, 22n
Titus, 64n
Tolstoy, Count Leo, 92

Verga, Giovanni, 11
Vigny, Count Alfred Victor de, 3
Voigt, Johannes, 45

Wedekind, Frank, 1
Whitehead, Alfred North, 85
Wild Duck, The, 15, 34
Wilde, Oscar, 1, 31
William I (the Conqueror), 87
Winters, Yvor, 97

COMPILED BY DAVID W. BEAMS